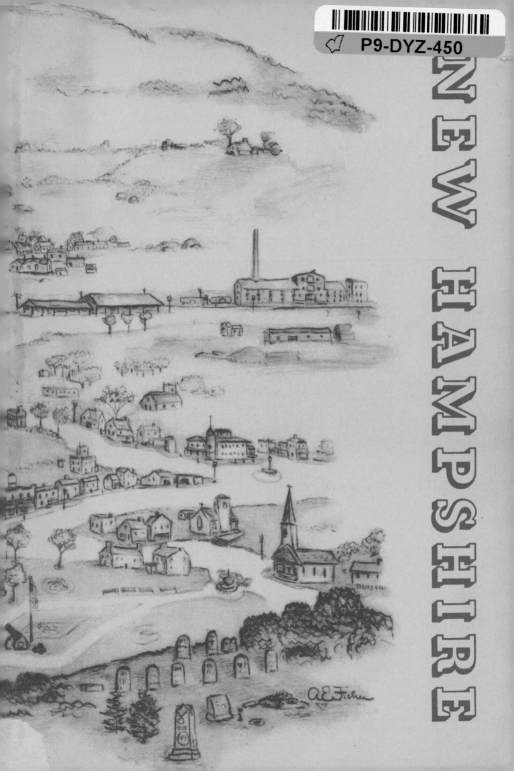

NEW HAMPSHIRE

A.E.Fisher

OUR TOWN

THE WORKS OF THORNTON WILDER

Novels

Collections of Short Plays

Plays

THORNTON WILDER

a play in three acts

New York·Coward McCann, Inc.

Designed by Robert Josephy

TO ALEXANDER WOOLLCOTT

of Castleton Township, Rutland County, Vermont

JED HARRIS

presents

OUR TOWN

A play by Thornton Wilder

WITH

FRANK CRAVEN

Production by Mr. Harris

Technical Direction by Raymond Sovey

Costumes Designed by Helene Pons

THE CAST *(in the order of their appearance)*

Stage Manager .... Frank Craven

Dr. Gibbs .... Jay Fassett

Joe Crowell .... Raymond Roe

Howie Newsome .... Tom Fadden

Mrs. Gibbs .... Evelyn Varden

Mrs. Webb .... Helen Carew

George Gibbs .... John Craven

Rebecca Gibbs .... Marilyn Erskine

Wally Webb .... Charles Wiley, Jr.

Emily Webb .... Martha Scott

Professor Willard .... Arthur Allen

Mr. Webb .... Thomas W. Ross

Woman in the Balcony .... Carrie Weller

Man in the Auditorium .... Walter O. Hill

Lady in the Box ....Aline McDermott
Simon Stimson ....Philip Coolidge
Mrs. Soames ....Doro Merande
Constable Warren ....E. Irving Locke
Si Crowell ....Billy Redfield
Baseball Players ....⎧ Alfred Ryder
⎨ William Roehrick
⎩ Thomas Coley
Sam Craig ....Francis G. Cleveland
Joe Stoddard ....William Wadsworth

People of the Town: Carrie Weller, Alice Donaldson,
Walter O. Hill, Arthur Allen, Charles Mellody,
Katharine Raht, Mary Elizabeth Forbes, Dorothy
Nolan, Jean Platt, Barbara Brown, Alda Stanley,
Barbara Burton, Lyn Swann, Dorothy Ryan, Shirley
Osborn, Emily Boileau, Ann Weston, Leon Rose,
John Irving Finn, Van Shem, Charles Walters,
William Short, Frank Howell, Max Beck, James
Malaidy.

The entire play takes place in Grover's Corners, N. H.,
1901 to 1913

Music arranged and organ played by Bernice Richmond

First performance at McCarter's Theatre, Princeton,
New Jersey, Jan. 22, 1938. First New York performance at the Henry Miller Theatre, Feb. 4, 1938.

ACT ONE

No curtain.

No scenery.

The audience, arriving, sees an empty stage in half-light.

Presently the STAGE MANAGER, *hat on and pipe in mouth, enters and begins placing a table and several chairs down stage left, and a table and chairs down stage right.*

"Left" and "right" are from the point of view of the actor facing the audience. "Up" is towards the back wall.

As the house lights go down he has finished setting the stage and leaning against the right proscenium pillar watches the late arrivals in the audience.

When the auditorium is in complete darkness he speaks:

STAGE MANAGER:

This play is called "Our Town." It was written by Thornton Wilder; produced and directed by A.... [or: produced by A....; directed by B....]. In it you will see Miss C....; Miss D....; Miss E....; and Mr. F....; Mr. G....; Mr. H....; and many others.

OUR TOWN

The name of the town is Grover's Corners, New Hampshire,—just across the Massachusetts line: longitude 42 degrees 40 minutes; latitude 70 degrees 37 minutes.

The First Act shows a day in our town. The day is May 7, 1901. The time is just before dawn.

A rooster crows.

The sky is beginning to show some streaks of light over in the East there, behind our mount'in.

The morning star always gets wonderful bright the minute before it has to go.

He stares at it for a moment, then goes up stage.

Well, I'd better show you how our town lies. Up here—

That is: parallel with the back wall.

is Main Street. Way back there is the railway station; tracks go that way. Polish Town's across the tracks and some Canuck families.

Toward the left:

Over there is the Congregational Church; across the street's the Presbyterian.

Methodist and Unitarian are over there.

Baptist is down in the holla' by the river.

Catholic Church is over beyond the tracks.

Here's the Town Hall and Post Office combined; jail's in the basement.

Bryan once made a speech from these steps here.

Along here's a row of stores. Hitching-posts and horse blocks in front of them. First automobile's going to come along in about five years,—belonged to Banker Cartwright, our richest citizen ... lives in the big white house up on the hill.

Here's the grocery store and here's Mr. Morgan's drug-store. Most everybody in town manages to look into those two stores once a day.

Public School's over yonder. High School's still farther over. Quarter of nine mornings, noontimes, and three o'clock afternoon's, the hull town can hear the yelling and screaming from those schoolyards.

> *He approaches the table and chairs down stage right:*

This is our doctor's house,—Doc Gibbs'. This is the back door.

> *Two arched trellises are pushed out, one by each proscenium pillar.*

There's some scenery for those who think they have to have scenery.

There's a garden here. Corn ... peas ... beans ... holly-hocks ... heliotrope ... and a lot of burdock.

> *Crosses the stage.*

In those days our newspaper come out twice a week,— The Grover's Corners *Sentinel,*—and this is Editor Webb's house.

And this is Mrs. Webb's garden.

Just like Mrs. Gibbs's, only it's got a lot of sunflowers, too.

Right here,—big butternut tree.

11

*He returns to his place by the right prosce-
nium pillar and looks at the audience for a
minute.*

Nice town, y'know what I mean?

Nobody very remarkable ever come out of it,—s'far
as we know.

The earliest tombstones in the cemetery up there on the
mountain say 1670-1680—they're Grovers and Cartwrights
and Gibbses and Herseys—same names as are around here
now.

Well, as I said: it's about dawn.

The only lights on in town are in a cottage over by the
tracks where a Polish mother's just had twins. And in the
Joe Crowell house, where Joe Junior's getting up so as to
deliver the paper. And in the depot, where Shorty
Hawkins is gettin' ready to flag the 5:45 for Boston.

A train whistle is heard. The STAGE MANAGER
takes out his watch and nods.

Naturally, out in the country—all around—they've been
lights on for some time, what with milkin's and so on.
But town people sleep late.

So—another day's begun.

There's Doc Gibbs comin' down Main Street now, comin'
back from that baby case. And here's his wife comin'
downstairs to get breakfast.

Doc Gibbs died in 1930. The new hospital's named after
him.

Mrs. Gibbs died first—long time ago in fact. She went out to visit her daughter, Rebecca, who married an insurance man in Canton, Ohio, and died there—pneumonia —but her body was brought back here. She's up in the cemetery there now—in with a whole mess of Gibbses and Herseys—she was Julia Hersey 'fore she married Doc Gibbs in the Congregational Church over there.

In our town we like to know the facts about everybody. —That's Doc Gibbs.

And there comes Joe Crowell, Jr., delivering Mr. Webb's *Sentinel*.

> DR. GIBBS *has been coming along Main Street from the left. At the point where he would turn to approach his house, he stops, sets down his—imaginary—black bag, takes off his hat, and rubs his face with fatigue, using an enormous handkerchief.*
>
> MRS. GIBBS *has entered her kitchen, gone through the motions of putting wood into a stove, lighting it, and preparing breakfast.*
>
> *Suddenly*, JOE CROWELL, JR., *starts down Main Street from the right, hurling imaginary newspapers into doorways.*

JOE CROWELL, JR.:

Morning, Doc Gibbs.

DR. GIBBS:

Morning, Joe.

13

JOE CROWELL, JR.:

Somebody been sick, Doc?

DR. GIBBS:

No. Just some twins born over in Polish Town.

JOE CROWELL, JR.:

Do you want your paper now?

DR. GIBBS:

Yes, I'll take it.—Anything serious goin' on in the world since Wednesday?

JOE CROWELL, JR.:

Yessir. My schoolteacher, Miss Foster, 's getting married to a fella over in Concord.

DR. GIBBS:

I declare.—How do you boys feel about that?

JOE CROWELL, JR.:

Well, of course, it's none of my business,—but I think if a person starts out to be a teacher, she ought to stay one.

DR. GIBBS:

How's your knee, Joe?

JOE CROWELL, JR.:

Fine, Doc, I never think about it at all. Only like you said, it always tells me when it's going to rain.

DR. GIBBS:

What's it telling you today? Goin' to rain?

JOE CROWELL, JR.:

No, sir.

14

DR. GIBBS:

Sure?

JOE CROWELL, JR.:

Yessir.

DR. GIBBS:

Knee ever make a mistake?

JOE CROWELL, JR.:

No, sir.

> JOE *goes off.* DR. GIBBS *stands reading his paper.*

STAGE MANAGER:

Here comes Howie Newsome delivering the milk.

> HOWIE NEWSOME *comes along Main Street,*
> *passes* DOCTOR GIBBS, *comes down the center of*
> *the stage, leaves some bottles at* MRS. WEBB'S
> *back door, and crosses the stage to* MRS.
> GIBBS'S.

HOWIE NEWSOME:

Git-ap, Bessie. What's the matter with you?—Morning, Doc.

DR. GIBBS:

Morning, Howie.

HOWIE NEWSOME:

Somebody sick?

DR. GIBBS:

Pair of twins over to Mrs. Goruslawski's.

HOWIE NEWSOME:

Twins, eh? This town's gettin' bigger every year.

15

DR. GIBBS:

Going to rain, Howie?

HOWIE NEWSOME:

No, no. Fine day—that'll burn through. Come on, Bessie.

DR. GIBBS:

Hello Bessie.

He strokes her.

How old is she, Howie?

HOWIE NEWSOME:

Going on seventeen. Bessie's all mixed up about the route ever since the Lockharts stopped takin' their quart of milk every day. She wants to leave 'em a quart just the same—keeps scolding me the hull trip.

He reaches MRS. GIBBS's *back door. She is waiting for him.*

MRS. GIBBS:

Good morning, Howie.

HOWIE NEWSOME:

Morning, Mrs. Gibbs. Doc's just comin' down the street.

MRS. GIBBS:

Is he? Seems like you're late today?

HOWIE NEWSOME:

Yes. Somep'n went wrong with the separator. Don't know what 'twas.

He goes back to Main Street, clucks for Bessie and goes off right.

DR. GIBBS *reaches his home and goes in.*

MRS. GIBBS:

Everything all right?

DR. GIBBS:

Yes. I declare—easy as kittens.

MRS. GIBBS:

Bacon'll be ready in a minute. Set down and drink your coffee. Child-*run!* Child-*run!* Time to get up.—George! Rebecca!—You can catch a couple hours' sleep this morning, can't you?

DR. GIBBS:

Hm! . . . Mrs. Wentworth's coming at eleven. Guess I know what it's about, too. Her stummick ain't what it ought to be.

MRS. GIBBS:

All told, you won't get more'n three hours' sleep. Frank Gibbs, I don't know what's goin' to become of you. I do wish I could get you to go away some place and take a rest. I think it would do you good.

MRS. WEBB:

Emileeee! Time to get up! Wally! Seven o'clock!

MRS. GIBBS:

I declare, you got to speak to George. Seems like something's come over him lately. He's no help to me at all. I can't even get him to cut me some wood.

DR. GIBBS:

Is he sassy to you?

MRS. GIBBS:

No. He just whines! All he thinks about is that baseball—
George! Rebecca! You'll be late for school.

DR. GIBBS:

M-m-m. . . .

MRS. GIBBS:

George!

DR. GIBBS:

George, look sharp!

GEORGE'S VOICE:

Yes, Pa!

DR. GIBBS:

As he goes off the stage.

Don't you hear your mother calling you?

MRS. WEBB:

Walleee! Emileee! You'll be late for school! Walleee!
You wash yourself good or I'll come up and do it myself.

REBECCA GIBBS'S VOICE:

Ma! What dress shall I wear?

MRS. GIBBS:

Don't make a noise. Your father's been out all night and
needs his sleep. I washed and ironed the blue gingham
for you special.

REBECCA:

Ma, I hate that dress.

18

MRS. GIBBS:

Oh, hush-up-with-you.

REBECCA:

Every day I go to school dressed like a sick turkey.

MRS. GIBBS:

Now, Rebecca, don't be impossible. You always look *very* nice.

REBECCA:

Mama, George's throwing soap at me.

MRS. GIBBS:

I'll come up and slap the both of you,—that's what I'll do.

> *A factory whistle sounds.*
> *The children enter and take their places at the breakfast tables:* EMILY and WALLY WEBB; GEORGE and REBECCA GIBBS.

STAGE MANAGER:

We've got a factory in our town too,—hear it? Makes blankets. Cartwrights own it and it brung 'em a fortune.

MRS. WEBB:

Children! Now I won't have it. Breakfast is just as good as any other meal and I won't have you gobbling like wolves. It'll stunt your growth,—that's a fact. Put away your book, Wally.

WALLY:

Aw, Ma!

MRS. WEBB:

You know the rule's well as I do—no books at table. As for me, I'd rather have my children healthy than bright.

EMILY:

I'm both, Mama: you know I am. I'm the brightest girl in school for my age. I have a wonderful memory.

MRS. WEBB:

Eat your breakfast.

WALLY:

I'm bright, too, when I'm looking at my stamp collection.

MRS. GIBBS:

I'll speak to your father about it when he's rested. Seems to me twenty-five cents a week's enough for a boy your age. I declare I don't know how you spend it all.

GEORGE:

Aw, Ma,—I gotta lotta things to buy.

MRS. GIBBS:

Strawberry phosphates—that's what you spend it on.

GEORGE:

I don't see how Rebecca comes to have so much money. She has more'n a dollar.

REBECCA:

Spoon in mouth, dreamily.

I've been saving it up gradual.

20

MRS. GIBBS:

Well, dear, I think it's a good thing every now and then to spend some.

REBECCA:

Mama, do you know what I love most in the world—do you?—Money.

MRS. GIBBS:

Eat your breakfast.

The school bell is heard.

THE CHILDREN:

Mama, there's first bell.—I gotta hurry.—I don't want any more.

MRS. WEBB:

Walk fast, but you don't have to run. Wally, pull up your pants at the knee. Stand up straight, Emily.

MRS. GIBBS:

Tell Miss Foster I send her my best congratulations—can you remember that?

REBECCA:

Yes, Ma.

MRS. GIBBS:

You look real nice, Rebecca. Pick up your feet.

ALL:

Good-by.

> *The children from the two houses join at the center of the stage and go up to Main Street, then off left.*

> MRS. GIBBS *fills her apron with food for the chickens and comes down to the footlights.*

MRS. GIBBS:

Here, chick, chick, chick.

No, go away, you. Go away.

Here, chick, chick, chick.

What's the matter with *you?* Fight, fight, fight,—that's all you do.

Hm . . . *you* don't belong to me. Where'd you come from?

> *She shakes her apron.*

Oh, don't be so scared. Nobody's going to hurt you.

> MRS. WEBB *is sitting by her trellis, stringing beans.*

MRS. GIBBS:

Good morning, Myrtle. How's your cold?

MRS. WEBB:

Well, it's better; but I told Charles I didn't know as I'd go to choir practice tonight. Wouldn't be any use.

MRS. GIBBS:

Just the same, you come to choir practice, Myrtle, and try it.

MRS. WEBB:

Well, if I don't feel any worse than I do now I probably will. While I'm resting myself I thought I'd string some of these beans.

MRS. GIBBS:

> *Rolling up her sleeves as she crosses the stage*
> *for a chat.*

Let me help you. Beans have been good this year.

MRS. WEBB:

I've decided to put up forty quarts if it kills me. The children say they hate 'em but I notice they're able to get 'em down all winter.

> *Pause.*

MRS. GIBBS:

Now, Myrtle. I've got to tell you something, because if I don't tell somebody I'll burst.

MRS. WEBB:

Why, Julia Gibbs!

MRS. GIBBS:

Here, give me some more of those beans. Myrtle, did one of those second-hand furniture men from Boston come to see you last Friday?

MRS. WEBB:

No—o.

MRS. GIBBS:

Well, he called on me. First I thought he was a patient wantin' to see Dr. Gibbs. 'N he wormed his way into my parlor, and, Myrtle Webb, he offered me three hundred and fifty dollars for Grandmother Wentworth's highboy, as I'm sitting here!

MRS. WEBB:

Why, Julia Gibbs!

MRS. GIBBS:

He did! That old thing! Why, it was so big I didn't know where to put it and I almost give it to Cousin Hester Wilcox.

MRS. WEBB:

Well, you're going to take it, aren't you?

MRS. GIBBS:

I don't know.

MRS. WEBB:

You don't know—three hundred and fifty dollars. What's come over you?

MRS. GIBBS:

Well, if I could get the Doctor to take the money and go away some place on a real trip I'd sell it like that.— Myrtle, ever since I was *that* high I've had the thought that I'd like to see Paris, France. I suppose I'm crazy.

MRS. WEBB:

Oh, I know what you mean.—How does the Doctor feel about it?

MRS. GIBBS:

Well, I did beat about the bush a little and said that if I got a legacy—that's the way I put it—I'd make him take me somewhere.

MRS. WEBB:

M-m-m. . . . What did he say?

MRS. GIBBS:

You know how he is. I haven't heard a serious word out
of him, ever since I've known him. No, he said, it might
make him discontented with Grover's Corners to go
traipsin' about Europe; better let well enough alone, he
says. Every two years he makes a trip to the battlefields
of the Civil War and that's enough treat for anybody,
he says.

MRS. WEBB:

Well, Mr. Webb just *admires* the way Dr. Gibbs knows
everything about the Civil War. Mr. Webb's a good mind
to give up Napoleon and move over to the Civil War,
only Dr. Gibbs being one of the greatest experts in the
country just makes him despair.

MRS. GIBBS:

It's a fact! Doctor Gibbs is never so happy as when he's
at Antietam or Gettysburg. The times I've walked over
those hills, Myrtle, stopping at every bush and pacing it
all out, like we was going to buy it.

MRS. WEBB:

Well, if that second-hand man's really serious about buyin'
it, Julia, you sell it. And then you'll get to see Paris, all
right.

MRS. GIBBS:

Oh, I'm sorry I mentioned it. Only it seems to me that
once in your life before you die you ought to see a

country where they don't talk and think in English and don't even want to.

The STAGE MANAGER *returns to the center of the stage.*

STAGE MANAGER:

That'll do. That'll do. Thank you very much, ladies.

MRS. GIBBS *and* MRS. WEBB *gather up their things, return into their homes and disappear.*

Now we're going to skip a few hours in the day at Grover's Corners.

But before we go on I want you to know some more things about the town,—all kinds of things.

So I've asked Prof. Willard of our State University to come down here and sketch in a few details of our past history,—kind of scientific account, you might say.

Is Prof. Willard here?

PROF. WILLARD, *a rural savant, pince-nez on a wide satin ribbon, enters from the right with some notes in his hand.*

May I introduce Prof. Willard of our University.

A few brief notes, thank you, Professor,—unfortunately our time is limited.

PROF. WILLARD:

Grover's Corners... let me see... Grover's Corners lies on the old Archaeozoic granite of the Appalachian range. I may say it's some of the oldest land in the world. We're very proud of that. A shelf of Devonian basalt

26

crosses it with vestiges of Mesozoic shale, and some sandstone outcroppings; but that's all more recent: two hundred, three hundred million years old.

Some highly interesting fossils have been found.... I may say: unique fossils ... two miles out of town, in Silas Peckham's cow pasture. They can be seen at the museum in our University at any time.

Did you wish the meteorological conditions?

STAGE MANAGER:

Thank you. We would.

PROF. WILLARD:

The mean precipitation is 40 inches. The mean annual temperature is 43 degrees, ranging between 102 degrees in the shade, and 38 degrees below zero in winter. The ... the ... uh ...

STAGE MANAGER:

Thank you, Professor. And have you Prof. Gruber's notes on the history of human life here?

PROF. WILLARD:

Hm ... yes ... anthropological data: Early Amerindian stock. Cotahatchee tribes ... no evidence before the Tenth Century of this era ... hm ... now entirely disappeared ... possible traces in three families. Migration toward the end of the Seventeenth Century of English brachycephalic blue-eyed stock ... for the most part. Since then some influx of Slav and Mediterranean types....

27

STAGE MANAGER:

And the population, Prof. Willard?

PROF. WILLARD:

Within the town limits: 2,640. The postal district brings in 507 more.

Mortality and birth-rates are constant; by MacPherson's gauge: 6.032.

STAGE MANAGER:

Thank you *very* much, Professor. We're all very much obliged to you, I'm sure.

PROF. WILLARD:

Not at all, sir; not at all.

STAGE MANAGER:

This way, Professor, and thank you again.

Exit PROF. WILLARD.

Now the political and social report: Editor Webb.—Oh, Mr. Webb?

MRS. WEBB *appears at her back door.*

MRS. WEBB:

He'll be here in a minute.... He just cut his hand while he was eatin' an apple.

STAGE MANAGER:

Thank you, Mrs. Webb.

MRS. WEBB:

Charles! Everybody's waitin'.

Exit MRS. WEBB.

STAGE MANAGER:

Mr. Webb is Publisher and Editor of The Grover's Corners *Sentinel.* That's our local paper, y'know.

> MR. WEBB *enters from his house, pulling on his coat. His finger is bound in a handkerchief.*

MR. WEBB:

Hm.... I don't have to tell you that we're run here by a Board of Selectmen.—All males vote at the age of 21. Women vote indirect. We're lower middle-class, sprinkling of professional men ... 10% illiterate laborers. Politically, we're 86% Republicans; 6% Democrats; 4% Socialists; rest, indifferent.

Religiously, we're 85% Protestants; 12% Catholics; rest, indifferent.

Do you want the poverty and insanity statistics?

STAGE MANAGER:

Thank you, no. Have you any comments, Mr. Webb?

MR. WEBB:

Very ordinary town, if you ask me. Little better behaved than most. Probably a lot duller.

But our young people here seem to like it well enough: 90% of 'em graduating from High School settle down right here to live—even when they've been away to college.

STAGE MANAGER:

Thank you, Mr. Webb. Now, is there anyone in the

audience who would like to ask Editor Webb anything about the town?

WOMAN IN THE BALCONY:

Is there much drinking in Grover's Corners?

MR. WEBB:

Well, ma'am, I wouldn't know what you'd call *much*. Satiddy nights the farmhands meet down in Ellery Greenough's stable and holler some. Fourth of July I've been known to taste a drop myself—and Decoration Day, of course. We've got one or two town drunks, but they're always having remorses every time an evangelist comes to town. No, ma'am, I'd say likker ain't a regular thing in the home here, except in the medicine chest. Right good for snake-bite, y'know—always was.

TALL MAN AT BACK OF AUDITORIUM:

Is there no one in town aware of—

STAGE MANAGER:

Come forward, will you, where we can all hear you— What were you saying?

TALL MAN:

Is there no one in town aware of social injustice and industrial inequality?

MR. WEBB:

Oh, yes, everybody is,—somethin' terrible. Seems like they spend most of their time talking about who's rich and who's poor.

30

TALL MAN:

Then why don't they do something about it?

MR. WEBB:

Well, we're ready to listen to everybody's suggestion as to how you can see that the diligent and sensible 'll rise to the top and the lazy and quarrelsome sink to the bottom. We'll listen to anybody. Meantime until that's settled, we try to take care of those that can't help themselves, and those that can we leave alone.—Are there any more questions?

LADY IN A BOX:

Oh, Mr. Webb? Mr. Webb, is there any culture or love of beauty in Grover's Corners?

MR. WEBB:

Well, ma'am, there ain't much—not in the sense you mean. Come to think of it, there's some girls that play the piano at High School Commencement; but they ain't happy about it. Yes, and I see where my daughter's been made to read "The Merchant of Venice" over to the school. Seems all pretty remote to 'em, y'know what I mean. No, ma'am, there isn't much culture; but maybe this is the place to tell you that we've got a lot of pleasures of a kind here: we like the sun comin' up over the mountain in the morning, and we all notice a good deal about the birds. We pay a lot of attention to them, and trees and plants. And we watch the change of the seasons: yes, everybody knows about them. But those other things—you're right, ma'am—there ain't much—"Robinson Crusoe" and the Bible; and Handel's "Largo," we all know that; and Whistler's "Mother"—those are just about as far as we go.

LADY IN A BOX:

So I thought. Thank you, Mr. Webb.

STAGE MANAGER:

All right! All right! Thank you, everybody.

> MR. WEBB *retires.*

We'll go back to the town now. It's middle of the afternoon. All 2,642 have had their dinners and all the dishes have been washed.

There's an early afternoon calm in our town: a buzzin' and a hummin' from the school buildings; only a few buggies on Main Street—the horses dozing at the hitching-posts; you all remember what it's like. Doc Gibbs is in his office, tapping people and making them say "ah." Mr. Webb's cuttin' his lawn over there; one man in ten thinks it's a privilege to push his own lawn mower.

No, sir. It's later than I thought. There are the children coming home from school already.

> EMILY WEBB *comes sedately down Main Street carrying some school books. There are some signs that she is imagining herself to be a lady of striking elegance.*
>
> *Her father's movements to and fro with the lawn mower bring him into her vicinity.*

32

EMILY:

I *can't*, Lois. I've got to go home and help my mother. I *promised.*

MR. WEBB:

Emily, walk simply. Who do you think you are today?

EMILY:

Papa, you're terrible. One minute you tell me to stand up straight and the next minute you call me names. I just don't listen to you.

She gives him an abrupt kiss.

MR. WEBB:

Golly, I never got a kiss from such a great lady before.

He goes out of sight. EMILY *leans over and picks some flowers by the gate of her house.* GEORGE GIBBS *comes careening down Main Street. He is throwing a ball up to dizzying heights, and waiting to catch it again. This sometimes requires his taking six steps backward.*

GEORGE:

Excuse me, Mrs. Forrest.

STAGE MANAGER (*as* MRS. FORREST):

Go out and play in the fields, young man. You got no business playing baseball on Main Street.

GEORGE:

Awfully sorry, Mrs. Forrest.—Hello, Emily.

33

EMILY:

H'lo.

GEORGE:

You made a fine speech in class.

EMILY:

Well...I was really ready to make a speech about the Monroe Doctrine, but at the last minute Miss Corcoran made me talk about the Louisiana Purchase instead. I worked an awful long time on both of them.

GEORGE:

Gee, it's funny, Emily. From my window up there I can just see your head nights when you're doing your home-work over in your room.

EMILY:

Why, can you?

GEORGE:

You certainly do stick to it, Emily. I don't see how you can sit still that long. I guess you like school.

EMILY:

Well, I always feel it's something you have to go through.

GEORGE:

Yeah.

EMILY:

I don't mind it really. It passes the time.

GEORGE:

Yeah.—Emily, what do you think? We might work out a kinda telegraph from there to there; and once in a while

you could give me a kinda hint or two about one of those
Algebra problems. I don't mean the answers, Emily, of
course not . . . just some little hint. . . .

EMILY:

Oh, I think *hints* are allowed.—So-ah—if you get stuck,
George, you whistle to me; and I'll give you some hints.

GEORGE:

Emily, you're just naturally bright, I guess.

EMILY:

I figure that it's just the way a person's born.

GEORGE:

Yeah. But, you see, I want to be a farmer, and my Uncle
Luke says whenever I'm ready I can come over and work
on his farm and if I'm any good I can just gradually have
it.

EMILY:

You mean the house and everything?

Enter MRS. WEBB.

GEORGE:

Yeah. Well, thanks . . . I better be getting out to the baseball field. Thanks for the talk, Emily.—Good afternoon,
Mrs. Webb.

MRS. WEBB:

Good afternoon, George.

GEORGE:

So-long, Emily.

EMILY:

So-long, George.

MRS. WEBB:

Emily, come and help me string these beans for the winter. George Gibbs let himself have a real conversation, didn't he? Why, he's growing up. How old would George be?

EMILY:

I don't know.

MRS. WEBB:

Let's see. He must be almost sixteen.

EMILY:

Mama, I made a speech in class today and I was very good.

MRS. WEBB:

You must recite it to your father at supper. What was it about?

EMILY:

The Louisiana Purchase. It was like silk off a spool. I'm going to make speeches all my life.—Mama, are these big enough?

MRS. WEBB:

Try and get them a little bigger if you can.

EMILY:

Mama, will you answer me a question, serious?

MRS. WEBB:

Seriously, dear—not serious.

36

EMILY:

Seriously,—will you?

MRS. WEBB:

Of course, I will.

EMILY:

Mama, am I good-looking?

MRS. WEBB:

Yes, of course you are. All my children have got good features; I'd be ashamed if they hadn't.

EMILY:

Oh, Mama, that's not what I mean. What I mean is: am I *pretty?*

MRS. WEBB:

I've already told you, yes. Now that's enough of that. You have a nice young pretty face. I never heard of such foolishness.

EMILY:

Oh, Mama, you never tell us the truth about anything.

MRS. WEBB:

I *am* telling you the truth.

EMILY:

Mama, were *you* pretty?

MRS. WEBB:

Yes, I was, if I do say it. I was the prettiest girl in town next to Mamie Cartwright.

EMILY:

But, Mama, you've got to say *some*thing about me. Am

37

I pretty enough . . . to get anybody . . . to get people interested in me?

MRS. WEBB:

Emily, you make me tired. Now stop it. You're pretty enough for all normal purposes. Come along now and bring that bowl with you.

EMILY:

Oh, Mama, you're no help at all.

STAGE MANAGER:

Thank you. Thank you! That'll do. We'll have to interrupt again here. Thank you, Mrs. Webb; thank you, Emily.

MRS. WEBB *and* EMILY *withdraw.*

There are some more things we've got to explore about this town.

This time we're going to go about it in another way: we're going to look back on it from the future.

I'm not going to tell you what became of these two families we're seeing most of, because the rest of the play will tell you about them.

But take some of these others:

Take Joe Crowell, Jr.:

Joe was a very bright fellow. He graduated with honors and got a scholarship to Boston Tech.,—M.I.T., that is. But the War broke out and Joe died in France. All that education for nothing.

38

Howie Newsome's still delivering milk at Grover's Corners. He's an old man now, has a lot of help, but he still delivers it himself. Says he gets the feel of the town that way. Carries all the accounts in his head; never has to write down a word.

Mr. Morgan's drug store ain't the same,—it's all citified. Mr. Morgan retired and went out to live in San Diego, California, where his daughter married a real estate man, name of Kerby. Mr. Morgan died there in 1935 and was buried in a lot of palm trees. Kinda lost his religion at the end and took up New Thought or something. They read some new-fangled poetry over him and cre-mated him. The New Hampshire in him sort of broke down in him in that climate, seems like.

The Cartwrights got richer and richer. The house is closed most of the year. They're off eating big dinners in hotels now,—in Virginia Hot Springs and Miami Beach. They say the winters are cold here. I see where they've become 'Piscopalians.

The Cartwright interests have just begun building a new bank in Grover's Corners—had to go to Vermont for the marble, sorry to say. And they've asked a friend of mine what they should put in the cornerstone for people to dig up a thousand years from now. Of course, they've put in a copy of the New York *Times* and a copy of Mr. Webb's *Sentinel*. We're kind of interested in this because some scientific fellas have found a way of painting all that read-

39

ing matter with a kind of glue—silicate glue—that'll make it keep a thousand—two thousand years.

We're putting in a Bible . . . and the Constitution of the United States and a copy of William Shakespeare's plays. What do you say, folks? What do you think?

Y'know—Babylon once had two million people in it, and all we know about 'em is the names of the kings and some copies of wheat contracts and . . . the sales of slaves. Yes, every night all those families sat down to supper, and the father came home from his work, and the smoke went up the chimney,—same as here. And even in Greece and Rome, all we know about the real life of the people is what we can piece together out of the joking poems and the comedies they wrote for the theater back then.

So I'm going to have a copy of this play put in the cornerstone and the people a thousand years from now'll know a few simple facts about us—more than the Treaty of Versailles and the Lindbergh flight.

See what I mean?

Well,—you people a thousand years from now,—in the provinces north of New York at the beginning of the Twentieth Century, people et three times a day: soon after sunrise; at noon; and at sunset.

Every seventh day, by law and by religion, was a day of rest and all work come to a stop.

The religion at that time was Christianity. I guess you have some other records about Christianity.

The domestic set-up was marriage: a binding relation between a male and one female that lasted for life.

Christianity strictly forbade killing, but you were allowed to kill animals, and you were allowed to kill human beings in war and government punishings.

I guess we don't have to tell you about the government and business forms, because that's the kind of thing people seem to hand down first of all.

Let me see now if there's anything else. Oh, yes,—at death people were buried in the ground just as they are.

So, friends, this is the way we were in our growing up and in our marrying and in our doctoring and in our living and in our dying.

Now we'll return to our day in Grover's Corners.

A lot of time has gone by. It's evening. You can hear choir practice going on in the Congregational Church. All the children are at home doing their school work. The day is running down like a tired clock.

> *A choir partially concealed in the orchestra pit has begun singing "Blessed be the tie that binds."*
>
> SIMON STIMSON *stands directing them.*
>
> *Two ladders have been pushed on to the stage; they serve as indication of the second story*

41

in the Gibbs and Webb houses. GEORGE *and*
EMILY *mount them, and apply themselves to
their school work.*

DR. GIBBS *has entered and is seated in his
kitchen reading.*

SIMON STIMSON:

Now look here, everybody. Music come into the world
to give pleasure.—Softer! Softer! Get it out of your heads
that music's only good when it's loud. You leave loud-
ness to the Methodists. You couldn't beat 'em, even if you
wanted to. Now again. Tenors!

GEORGE:

Hssst! Emily!

EMILY:

Hello.

GEORGE:

Hello!

EMILY:

I can't work at all. The moonlight's so *terrible.*

GEORGE:

Emily, did you get the third problem?

EMILY:

Which?

GEORGE:

The *third?*

EMILY:

Why, yes, George—that's the easiest of them all.

42

GEORGE:

I don't see it. Emily, can you give me a hint?

EMILY:

I'll tell you one thing: the answer's in yards.

GEORGE:

!!! In yards? How do you mean?

EMILY:

In *square* yards.

GEORGE:

Oh . . . in square yards.

EMILY:

Yes, George, don't you see?

GEORGE:

Yeah.

EMILY:

In square yards of *wallpaper.*

GEORGE:

Wallpaper,—oh, I see. Thanks a lot, Emily.

EMILY:

You're welcome. My, isn't the moonlight *terrible?* And choir practice going on.—I think if you hold your breath you can hear the train all the way to Contookuck. Hear it?

GEORGE:

M-m-m—What do you know!

EMILY:

Well, I guess I better go back and try to work.

GEORGE:

Good night, Emily. And thanks.

EMILY:

Good night, George.

SIMON STIMSON:

Before I forget it: how many of you will be able to come in Tuesday afternoon and sing at Fred Hersey's wedding, —show your hands. That'll be fine; that'll be right nice. We'll do the same music we did for Jane Trowbridge's last month.

—Now we'll do: "Art thou weary; art thou languid?" It's a question, ladies and gentlemen, make it talk. Ready.

DR. GIBBS:

Oh, George, can you come down a minute?

GEORGE:

Yes, Pa.

He descends the ladder.

DR. GIBBS:

Make yourself comfortable, George; I'll only keep you a minute. George, how old are you?

GEORGE:

I? I'm sixteen, almost seventeen.

DR. GIBBS:

What do you want to do after school's over?

GEORGE:

Why, you know, Pa, I want to be a farmer on Uncle Luke's farm.

44

DR. GIBBS:

You'll be willing, will you, to get up early and milk and feed the stock . . . and you'll be able to hoe and hay all day?

GEORGE:

Sure, I will. What are you . . . what do you mean, Pa?

DR. GIBBS:

Well, George, while I was in my office today I heard a funny sound . . . and what do you think it was? It was your mother chopping wood. There you see your mother —getting up early; cooking meals all day long; washing and ironing;—and still she has to go out in the back yard and chop wood. I suppose she just got tired of asking you. She just gave up and decided it was easier to do it herself. And you eat her meals, and put on the clothes she keeps nice for you, and you run off and play baseball, —like she's some hired girl we keep around the house but that we don't like very much. Well, I knew all I had to do was call your attention to it. Here's a handkerchief, son. George, I've decided to raise your spending money twenty-five cents a week. Not, of course, for chopping wood for your mother, because that's a present you give her, but because you're getting older—and I imagine there are lots of things you must find to do with it.

GEORGE:

Thanks, Pa.

DR. GIBBS:

Let's see—tomorrow's pay day. You can count on it—
Hmm. Probably Rebecca'll feel she ought to have some
more too. Wonder what could have happened to your
mother. Choir practice never was as late as this before.

GEORGE:

It's only half-past eight, Pa.

DR. GIBBS:

I don't know why she's in that old choir. She hasn't any
more voice than an old crow.... Traipsin' around the
streets at this hour of the night.... Just about time you
retired, don't you think?

GEORGE:

Yes, Pa.

> GEORGE *mounts to his place on the ladder.*
> *Laughter and good nights can be heard on*
> *stage left and presently* MRS. GIBBS, MRS.
> SOAMES *and* MRS. WEBB *come down Main*
> *Street. When they arrive at the center of the*
> *stage they stop.*

MRS. SOAMES:

Good night, Martha. Good night, Mr. Foster.

MRS. WEBB:

I'll tell Mr. Webb; I *know* he'll want to put it in the
paper.

MRS. GIBBS:

My, it's late!

46

MRS. SOAMES:

Good night, Irma.

MRS. GIBBS:

Real nice choir practice, wa'n't it? Myrtle Webb! Look at that moon, will you! Tsk-tsk-tsk. Potato weather, for sure.

MRS. SOAMES:

Naturally I didn't want to say a word about it in front of those others, but now we're alone—really, it's the worst scandal that ever was in this town!

MRS. GIBBS:

What?

MRS. SOAMES:

Simon Stimson!

MRS. GIBBS:

Now, Louella!

MRS. SOAMES:

But, Julia! To have the organist of a church drink and drunk year after year. You know he was drunk to-night.

MRS. GIBBS:

Now, Louella! We all know about Mr. Stimson, and we all know about the troubles he's been through, and Dr. Ferguson knows too, and if Dr. Ferguson keeps him on there in his job the only thing the rest of us can do is just not to notice it.

47

MRS. SOAMES:

Not to notice it! But it's getting worse.

MRS. WEBB:

No, it isn't, Louella. It's getting better. I've been in that choir twice as long as you have. It doesn't happen anywhere near so often.... My, I hate to go to bed on a night like this.—I better hurry. Those children'll be sitting up till all hours. Good night, Louella.

> *She hurries down stage, enters her house and disappears.*

MRS. GIBBS:

Can you get home safe, Louella?

MRS. SOAMES:

It's as bright as day. I can see Mr. Soames scowling at the window now. You'd think we'd been to a dance the way the menfolk carry on.

> *Repeated good nights.* MRS. GIBBS *arrives at her home.*

MRS. GIBBS:

Well, we had a real good time.

DR. GIBBS:

You're late enough.

MRS. GIBBS:

Why, Frank, it ain't any later 'n usual.

DR. GIBBS:

And you stopping at the corner to gossip with a lot of hens.

48

MRS. GIBBS:

Now, Frank, don't be grouchy. Come out and smell my heliotrope in the moonlight.

> *They stroll out arm in arm along the footlights.*

Isn't that wonderful? What did you do all the time I was away?

DR. GIBBS:

Oh, I read—as usual. What were the girls gossiping about tonight?

MRS. GIBBS:

Well, believe me, Frank—there is something to gossip about.

DR. GIBBS:

Hmm! Simon Stimson far gone, was he?

MRS. GIBBS:

Worst I've ever seen him. How'll that end, Frank? Dr. Ferguson can't forgive him forever.

DR. GIBBS:

I guess I know more about Simon Stimson's affairs than anybody in this town. Some people ain't made for small town life. I don't know how that'll end; but there's nothing we can do but just leave it alone. Come, get in.

MRS. GIBBS:

No, not yet. . . . Oh, Frank, I'm worried about you.

DR. GIBBS:

What are you worried about?

MRS. GIBBS:

I think it's my duty to make plans for you to get a real rest and change. And if I get that legacy, well, I'm going to insist on it.

DR. GIBBS:

Now, Julia, there's no sense in going over that again.

MRS. GIBBS:

Frank, you're just *unreasonable!*

DR. GIBBS:

Come on, Julia, it's getting late. First thing you know you'll catch cold. I gave George a piece of my mind tonight. I reckon you'll have your wood chopped for a while anyway. No, no, start getting upstairs.

MRS. GIBBS:

Oh, dear. There's always so many things to pick up, seems like. You know, Frank, Mrs. Fairchild always locks her front door every night. All those people up that part of town do.

DR. GIBBS:

They're all getting citified, that's the trouble with them. They haven't got nothing fit to burgle and everybody knows it.

> *They disappear.*
>
> REBECCA *climbs up the ladder beside* GEORGE.

GEORGE:

Get out, Rebecca. There's only room for one at this window. You're always spoiling everything.

50

REBECCA:

Well, let me look just a minute.

GEORGE:

Use your own window.

REBECCA:

I did; but there's no moon there. . . . George, do you know what I think, do you? I think maybe the moon's getting nearer and nearer and there'll be a big 'splosion.

GEORGE:

Rebecca, you don't know anything. If the moon were getting nearer, the guys that sit up all night with telescopes would see it first and they'd tell about it, and it'd be in all the newspapers.

REBECCA:

George, is the moon shining on South America, Canada and half the whole world?

GEORGE:

Well—prob'ly is.

The STAGE MANAGER *strolls on.*

STAGE MANAGER:

Nine-thirty. Most of the lights are out. No, there's Constable Warren trying a few doors on Main Street. And here comes Editor Webb, after putting his newspaper to bed.

MR. WEBB:

Good evening, Bill.

CONSTABLE WARREN:

Evenin', Mr. Webb.

MR. WEBB:

Quite a moon!

CONSTABLE WARREN:

Yepp.

MR. WEBB:

All quiet tonight?

CONSTABLE WARREN:

Simon Stimson is rollin' around a little. Just saw his wife movin' out to hunt for him so I looked the other way— there he is now.

> SIMON STIMSON *comes down Main Street from the left, only a trace of unsteadiness in his walk.*

MR. WEBB:

Good evening, Simon.... Town seems to have settled down for the night pretty well....

> SIMON STIMSON *comes up to him and pauses a moment.*

Good evening.... Yes, most of the town's settled down for the night, Simon.... I guess we better do the same. Can I walk along a ways with you?

> SIMON STIMSON *continues on his way without a word and disappears at the right.*

Good night.

CONSTABLE WARREN:

I don't know how that's goin' to end, Mr. Webb.

MR. WEBB:

Well, he's seen a peck of trouble, one thing after another.... Oh, Bill... if you see my boy smoking cigarettes, just give him a word, will you? He thinks a lot of you, Bill.

CONSTABLE WARREN:

I don't think he smokes no cigarettes, Mr. Webb. Leastways, not more'n two or three a year. He don't belong to that crowd that hangs out down by the gully.

MR. WEBB:

Hm. . . . I hope not.—Well, good night, Bill.

CONSTABLE WARREN:

Good night, Mr. Webb.

> *Exit.*

MR. WEBB:

Who's that up there? Is that you, Myrtle?

EMILY:

No, it's me, Papa.

MR. WEBB:

Why aren't you in bed?

EMILY:

I don't know. I just can't sleep yet, Papa. The moonlight's so *won*-derful. And the smell of Mrs. Gibbs' heliotrope. Can you smell it?

MR. WEBB:

Hm. ... Yes. Haven't any troubles on your mind, have you, Emily?

EMILY:

Troubles, Papa. *No.*

MR. WEBB:

Well, enjoy yourself, but don't let your mother catch you. Good night, Emily.

EMILY:

Good night, Papa.

> MR. WEBB *crosses into the house, whistling "Blessed Be the Tie that Binds" and disappears.*

REBECCA:

I never told you about that letter Jane Crofut got from her minister when she was sick. The minister of her church in the town she was in before she came here. He wrote Jane a letter and on the envelope the address was like this: It said: Jane Crofut; The Crofut Farm; Grover's Corners; Sutton County; New Hampshire; United States of America.

GEORGE:

What's funny about that?

REBECCA:

But listen, it's not finished: the United States of America; Continent of North America; Western Hemisphere; the Earth; the Solar System; the Universe; the Mind of God, —that's what it said on the envelope.

54

GEORGE:

What do you know!

REBECCA:

And the postman brought it just the same.

GEORGE:

What do you know!

STAGE MANAGER:

That's the end of the First Act, friends. You can go and smoke now, those that smoke.

ACT TWO

*The tables and chairs of the two kitchens are
still on the stage.*
The ladders have been withdrawn.
The STAGE MANAGER *has been at his accustomed place watching the audience return to
its seats.*

STAGE MANAGER:

Three years have gone by.

Yes, the sun's come up over a thousand times.

Summers and winters have cracked the mountains a little
bit more and the rains have brought down some of the
dirt.

Some babies that weren't even born before have begun
talking regular sentences already; and a number of people
who thought they were right young and spry have noticed that they can't bound up a flight of stairs like they
used to, without their heart fluttering a little.

Some older sons are sitting at the head of the table, and
some people I know are having their meat cut up for
them.—

All that can happen in a thousand days.

Nature's been pushing and contriving in other ways, too:
a number of young people fell in love and got married.

56

Yes, the mountain got bit away a few fractions of an inch; millions of gallons of water went by the mill; and here and there a new home was set up under a roof.

Almost everybody in the world gets married,—you know what I mean? In our town there aren't hardly any exceptions. Most everybody in the world climbs into their graves married.

The First Act was called the Daily Life. This Act is called Love and Marriage. There's another Act coming after this: I reckon you can guess what that's about.

So:

It's three years later. It's 1904.

It's July 7th, just after High School Commencement. That's the time most of our young people jump up and get married. Soon as they've passed their last examinations in solid geometry and Cicero's Orations, looks like they suddenly feel themselves fit to be married.

It's early morning. Only this time it's been raining. It's been pouring and thundering.

Mrs. Gibbs's garden, and Mrs. Webb's here: drenched.

All those bean poles and pea vines: drenched.

All yesterday over there on Main Street, the rain looked like curtains being blown along.

Hm...it may begin again any minute.

There! You can hear the 5:45 for Boston.

And here comes Howie Newsome delivering the milk.

And there's Si Crowell delivering the papers like his

brother before him.—You remember about his brother?—
all that education he's going to get and that'll be wasted.
And there's Mrs. Gibbs and Mrs. Webb come down to
make breakfast, just as though it were an ordinary day.
I don't have to point out to the women in my audience
that those ladies they see before them, both those ladies
cooked three meals a day,—one of 'em for twenty years,
the other for forty,—and no summer vacation. They
brought up two children apiece; washed; cleaned the
house,—and never a nervous breakdown. Never thought
themselves hard-used, either.

It's like what one of those Middle West poets said: You've
got to love life to have life, and you've got to have life
to love life.... It's what they call a vicious circle.

> SI CROWELL *has entered hurling imaginary*
> *newspapers into doorways;* HOWIE NEWSOME
> *has come along Main Street with* BESSIE.

HOWIE NEWSOME:

Git-ap, Bessie.

SI CROWELL:

Morning, Howie.

HOWIE NEWSOME:

Morning, Si.—Anything in the papers I ought to know?

SI CROWELL:

Nothing much, except we're losing about the best baseball pitcher Grover's Corners ever had.

58

HOWIE NEWSOME:

Reckon he was. He's been standing off the whole of South New Hampshire single-handed, looks like.

SI CROWELL:

He could hit and run bases, too.

HOWIE NEWSOME:

Yep. Mighty fine ball player.—Bessie! I guess I can stop and talk if I've a mind to!

SI CROWELL:

I don't see how he could give up a thing like that just to get married. Would you, Howie?

HOWIE NEWSOME:

Can't tell, Si. Never had no talent that way.

> CONSTABLE WARREN *enters. They exchange mornings.*

You're up early, Bill.

CONSTABLE WARREN:

Seein' if there's anything I can do to prevent a flood. River's been risin' all night.

HOWIE NEWSOME:

Si Crowell's all worked up here about George Gibbs' retiring from baseball.

CONSTABLE WARREN:

Yes, sir; that's the way it goes. Back in '84 we had a player, Si,—even George Gibbs couldn't touch him. Name of Hank Todd. Went down to Maine and become a parson.

Wonderful ball player.—Howie, how did the weather look to you?

HOWIE NEWSOME:

No, 'tain't bad. Think maybe it'll clear up for good.

> CONSTABLE WARREN *and* SI CROWELL *continue on their way.*
>
> HOWIE NEWSOME *brings the milk first to* MRS. GIBBS'S *house. She meets him by the trellis.*

MRS. GIBBS:

Good morning, Howie. Do you think it's going to rain again?

HOWIE NEWSOME:

Morning, Mrs. Gibbs. It rained so heavy, I think maybe it'll clear up.

MRS. GIBBS:

Certainly hope it will.

HOWIE NEWSOME:

How much did you want today?

MRS. GIBBS:

I guess I'll need three-a-milk and two-a-cream, Howie. I'm going to have a house full of relations.

HOWIE NEWSOME:

My wife says to tell you we both hope they'll be very happy, Mrs. Gibbs. Know they *will.*

MRS. GIBBS:

Thanks a lot, Howie. Tell your wife I hope she gits there to the wedding.

60

HOWIE NEWSOME:

Yes, she'll be there; she'll be there if she kin.

> HOWIE NEWSOME *crosses to* MRS. WEBB'S *house.*

Morning, Mrs. Webb.

MRS. WEBB:

Oh, good morning, Mr. Newsome. I told you four quarts of milk, but I hope you can spare me another.

HOWIE NEWSOME:

Yes'm... and the two of cream.

MRS. WEBB:

Will it rain all day, Mr. Newsome?

HOWIE NEWSOME:

No'm. Just sayin' to Mrs. Gibbs as how it may lighten up. Mrs. Newsome told me to tell you as how we hope they'll both be very happy, Mrs. Webb. Know they *will.*

MRS. WEBB:

Thank you, and thank Mrs. Newsome and we hope to see you all at the wedding.

HOWIE NEWSOME:

Yes, Mrs. Webb. We hope to git there. Couldn't miss that. Chck! Bessie!

> *Exit* HOWIE NEWSOME.
>
> DR. GIBBS *descends in shirt sleeves, and sits down at his breakfast table.*

DR. GIBBS:

Well, Ma, the day has come. You're losin' one of your chicks.

61

MRS. GIBBS:

Frank Gibbs, don't you say another word. I feel like crying every minute. Sit down and drink your coffee.

DR. GIBBS:

The groom's up shaving himself. Whistling and singing, like he's glad to leave us.—Every now and then he says "I do" to the mirror, but it don't sound convincing to me.

MRS. GIBBS:

I declare I don't know how he'll get along. I've arranged his clothes and seen to it he's put warm things on,— Frank! they're too young. Emily won't think of such things. He'll catch his death of cold within a week.— Here's something I made for you.

DR. GIBBS:

Why, Julia Hersey! French toast!

MRS. GIBBS:

'Tain't hard to make, and I had to do something.

DR. GIBBS:

I remember my wedding morning, Julia.

MRS. GIBBS:

Now don't start that, Frank Gibbs. I tell you I can't stand it.

DR. GIBBS:

I was the scardest young fella in the State of New Hampshire. I thought I'd made a mistake for sure. And when I saw you comin' down that aisle I thought you were the prettiest girl I'd ever seen, but the only trouble was that I'd never seen you before. There I was in the Congregational Church marryin' a total stranger.

MRS. GIBBS:

And how do you think I felt!—Did you hear Rebecca stirring about upstairs?

DR. GIBBS:

Only morning in the year she hasn't been managing everybody's business. She's shut up in her room. I got the impression that maybe she's crying.

MRS. GIBBS:

Good Lord! This has got to stop.—Rebecca! Rebecca! Everything's getting cold down here.

> GEORGE *comes rattling down the stairs, very brisk.*

GEORGE:

Good morning, everybody. Only five more hours to live.
Makes the gesture of cutting his throat.

MRS. GIBBS:

Where are you going?

GEORGE:

Just stepping across the grass to see my girl.

MRS. GIBBS:

Now, George! You take an umbrella or I won't let you out of this house.

GEORGE:

Aw, Ma. It's just a *step!*

MRS. GIBBS:

From tomorrow on you can kill yourself in all weathers, but while you're in my house you live wisely, thank you. There are your overshoes right there in the hall. And here's an umbrella.

GEORGE:

Aw, Ma!

DR. GIBBS:

George, do as your mother tells you.

MRS. GIBBS:

Maybe Mrs. Webb isn't used to callers at seven in the morning. Take a cup-a coffee first.

GEORGE:

Be back in a minute.

> *He crosses the stage, leaping over the puddles.*

Good morning, Mother Webb.

MRS. WEBB:

Goodness! You frightened me!—Now, George, you can come in a minute out of the wet, but you know I can't ask you in.

GEORGE:

Why not—?

MRS. WEBB:

George, you know's well as I do: the groom can't see

his bride on his wedding day, not until he sees her in church.

GEORGE:

Aw!—that's just a superstition.

Enter MR. WEBB.

MR. WEBB:

Good morning, George.

GEORGE:

Mr. Webb, you don't believe in that superstition, do you?

MR. WEBB:

There's a lot of common sense in some superstitions, George.

MRS. WEBB:

Millions have folla'd it, George, and you don't want to be the first to fly in the face of custom.

GEORGE:

How is Emily?

MRS. WEBB:

She hasn't waked up yet. I haven't heard a sound out of her.

GEORGE:

Emily's *asleep!!!*

MRS. WEBB:

No wonder! We were up 'til all hours,—sewing and packing. I'll tell you what I'll do; you set down here a minute with Mr. Webb and drink this cup of coffee; and I'll go

65

upstairs and see she doesn't come down and surprise you. There's some bacon, too; but don't be long about it.

Exit MRS. WEBB.

Embarrassed silence.

MR. WEBB:

Well, George, how are you?

GEORGE:

Oh, fine. I'm fine.

Pause.

Mr. Webb, what sense could there be in a superstition like that?

MR. WEBB:

Well, you see,—on her wedding morning a girl's head's apt to be full of . . . clothes and things like that. Don't you think that's probably it?

GEORGE:

Ye-e-s. I never thought of that.

MR. WEBB:

A girl's apt to be a mite nervous on her wedding day.

Pause.

GEORGE:

I wish a fellow could get married without all that marching up and down.

MR. WEBB:

Well, every man that's ever lived has felt that way about it, George; but it hasn't done much good. It's the women that have built up weddings, my boy. From now on they

66

have it pretty much as they like.... All those good women standing shoulder to shoulder making sure that the knot's tied in a mighty public way.

GEORGE:

But...you *believe* in it, don't you, Mr. Webb?

MR. WEBB:

Oh, yes; oh, yes. Don't you misunderstand me, my boy. Marriage is a wonderful thing,—wonderful thing. And don't you forget that, George.

GEORGE:

No, sir.—Mr. Webb, how old were you when you got married?

MR. WEBB:

Well, you see: I'd been to college and I'd taken a little time to get settled. But Mrs. Webb,—she wasn't much older than what Emily is. Oh, age hasn't much to do with it, George,—not compared to other things.

GEORGE:

What were you going to say, Mr. Webb?

MR. WEBB:

Oh, I don't know,—was I going to say something?
        Pause.

George, I was thinking the other night of some advice my father gave me when I got married. Charles, he said, Charles, start out early showing who's boss, he said. Best thing to do is to give an order, even if it don't make sense; just so she'll learn to obey. And he said: if anything about your wife irritates you,—her conversation, or anything,—just get up and leave the house. That'll make it clear to her, he said. And, oh, yes! he said never, *never* let your wife know how much money you have, never.

GEORGE:

Well, Mr. Webb...I don't think I could...

MR. WEBB:

So I took the opposite of my father's advice and I've been happy ever since. And let that be a lesson to you, George, never to ask advice on personal matters.—George, are you going to raise chickens on your farm?

GEORGE:

What?

MR. WEBB:

Are you going to raise chickens on your farm?

GEORGE:

Uncle Luke's never been much interested, but I thought—

MR. WEBB:

A book came into my office the other day, George, on the Philo System of raising chickens. I want you to read it. I'm thinking of beginning in a small way in the back yard, and I'm going to put an incubator in the cellar—

Enter MRS. WEBB.

MRS. WEBB:

Charles, are you talking about that old incubator again? I thought you two'd be talking about things worth while.

68

MR. WEBB:

Well, Myrtle, if you want to give the boy some good advice, I'll go upstairs and leave you alone with him.

MRS. WEBB:

Now, George, I'm sorry, but I've got to send you away so that Emily can come down and get some breakfast. She told me to tell you that she sends you her love but that she doesn't want to lay eyes on you. So good-by, George.

> GEORGE *crosses the stage to his own home and disappears.*

MR. WEBB:

Myrtle, I guess you don't know about that older superstition.

MRS. WEBB:

What do you mean, Charles?

MR. WEBB:

Since the cave-men: the groom shouldn't be left alone with his father-in-law on the day of the wedding, or near it. Now don't forget that!

STAGE MANAGER:

Thank you. Thank you, everybody. Now I have to interrupt again here. You see, we want to know how all this began,—this wedding, this plan to spend a lifetime together. I'm awfully interested in how big things like that begin.

You know how it is: you're twenty-one or twenty-two

and you make some decisions; then whisssh! you're seventy: you've been a lawyer for fifty years, and that white-haired lady at your side has eaten over fifty thousand meals with you.

How do such things begin? *now there was a moment when this all began*

George and Emily are going to show you now the conversation they had when they first knew that... that... as the saying goes... they were meant for one another.

But before we show it to you we want you out there to do something for us we —

But before they do it I want you to try and remember what it was like when you were young, *going* when you were fifteen or sixteen. For some reason it is very hard to do: those days when even the little things in life could be almost too exciting to bear.

Remember from

And particularly the days when you were first in love; when you were like a person sleep-walking, and you didn't quite see the street you were in, and didn't quite hear everything that was said to you.

You're just a little bit crazy. Will you remember that, please? *It all happens on the way home from School*

Now they'll be coming out of High School at three o'clock. George has just been elected President of the Junior Class, and as it's June, that means he'll be President of the Senior Class all next year. And Emily's just been elected Secretary and Treasurer.

I don't have to tell you how important that is.

He places a board across the backs of two chairs, parallel to the footlights, and places two

70

Here they are coming down main St now.

high stools behind it. This is the counter of
MR. MORGAN'S *drugstore.*

All ready!

> EMILY, *carrying an armful of—imaginary—*
> *school-books, comes along Main Street from*
> *the left.*

EMILY:

I can't, Louise. I've got to go home. Good-by.

Oh, Earnestine! Earnestine! Can you come over tonight
and do Algebra? I did the first and third in Study Hall.
No, they're not hard. But, Earnestine, that Caesar's awful
hard. I don't see why we have to do a thing like that.
Come over about seven. Tell your mother you *have* to.
G'by.

G'by, Helen. G'by, Fred.

> GEORGE, *also carrying books, catches up with*
> *her.*

GEORGE:

Can I carry your books home for you, Emily?

EMILY:

> *Coldly.*

Thank you.

> *She gives them to him.*

GEORGE:

Excuse me a minute, Emily.—Say, Bob, get everything
ready. I'll be there in a quarter of an hour. If I'm a little

71

late start practice anyway. And give Herb some long high ones. His eye needs a lot of practice. Seeya later.

EMILY:

Good-by, Lizzy.

GEORGE:

Good-by, Lizzy.—I'm awfully glad you were elected, too, Emily.

EMILY:

Thank you.

> *They have been standing on Main Street, almost against the back wall.* GEORGE *is about to take the first steps towards the audience when he stops again and says:*

GEORGE:

Emily, why are you mad at me?

EMILY:

I'm not mad at you.

GEORGE:

You . . . you treat me so funny.

EMILY:

Well, I might as well say it right out, George. I don't like the whole change that's come over you in the last year. I'm sorry if that hurts your feelings, but I've just got to tell the truth and shame the devil.

GEORGE:

I'm awfully sorry, Emily. Wha-a-what do you mean?

72

EMILY:

Well, up to a year ago I used to like you a lot. And I
used to watch you as you did everything ... because we'd
been friends so long ... and then you began spending all
your time at baseball ... and you never even spoke to
anybody any more; not even to your own family you
didn't ... and, George, it's a fact, you've got awful con-
ceited and stuck-up, and all the girls say so. They may
not say so to your face, but that's what they say about
you behind your back, and it hurts me to hear them say
it, but I've got to agree with them a little. I'm sorry if it
hurts your feelings ... but I can't be sorry I said it.

GEORGE:

I ... I'm glad you said it, Emily. I never thought that
such a thing was happening to me. I guess it's hard for a
fella not to have faults creep into his character.

> *They take a step or two in silence, then stand
> still in misery.*

EMILY:

I always expect a man to be perfect and I think he should
be.

GEORGE:

Oh ... I don't think it's possible to be perfect, Emily.

EMILY:

Well, my father is, and as far as I can see your father is.
There's no reason on earth why you shouldn't be, too.

GEORGE:

Well, Emily ... I feel it's the other way round. That men aren't naturally good; but girls are. Like you and your mother and my mother.

EMILY:

Well, you might as well know right now that I'm not perfect. It's not as easy for a girl to be perfect as a man, because we girls are more nervous.—Now I'm sorry I said all that about you. I don't know what made me say it.

GEORGE:

No, no,—I guess if it's the truth you ought to say it. You stick to it, Emily.

EMILY:

I don't know if it's the truth or not. And I suddenly feel that it isn't important at all.

GEORGE:

Emily, would you like an ice-cream soda, or something, before you go home?

EMILY:

Well, thank you.... I would.

> *They come into the drugstore and seat themselves on the stools.*

STAGE MANAGER (*as* MR. MORGAN):

Hello, George. Hello, Emily. What'll you have? Why, Emily Webb, what've you been crying about?

74

GEORGE:

He gropes for an explanation.

She . . . she just got an awful scare, Mr. Morgan. She almost got run over by that hardware store wagon. Everybody always says that Tom Huckins drives like a crazy man.

STAGE MANAGER:

Here, take a drink of water, Emily. You look all shook up. There!—Now, what'll you have?

EMILY:

I'll have a strawberry phosphate, thank you, Mr. Morgan.

GEORGE:

No, no. You go and have an ice-cream soda with me, Emily.—Two strawberry ice-cream sodas, Mr. Morgan.

STAGE MANAGER:

Working the faucets.

Yes, sir. I tell you, you've got to look both ways before you cross Main Street these days. Gets worse every year. There are a hundred and twenty-five horses in Grover's Corners this minute I'm talking to you. State Inspector was in here yesterday. And now they're bringing in these auto-mo-biles, the best thing to do is to just stay home. Why, I can remember the time when a dog could lie down all day in the middle of Main Street and nothing would come to disturb him.—Yes, Miss Ellis; be with you in a minute. Here are your sodas. Enjoy 'em.

He goes off.

75

EMILY:

They're so expensive.

GEORGE:

No, no,—don't you think of that. We're celebrating. First, we're celebrating our election. And then do you know what else I'm celebrating?

EMILY:

No.

GEORGE:

I'm celebrating because I've got a friend who tells me all the things that ought to be told me.

EMILY:

George, *please* don't think of that. I don't know why I said it. It's not true. You're—

GEORGE:

No, you stick to it, Emily. I'm glad you spoke to me like you did. But you'll see: I'm going to change so quick— you bet I'm going to change. And, Emily, I want to ask you a favor.

EMILY:

What?

GEORGE:

Emily, if I go away to State Agriculture College next year, will you write me a letter once in a while?

EMILY:

I certainly will. I certainly will, George. . . .

> *Pause.*

It certainly seems like being away three years you'd get out of touch with things.

GEORGE:

No, no. I mustn't do that. You see I'm not only going to be just a farmer. After a while maybe I'll run for something to get elected. So your letters'll be very important to me; you know, telling me what's going on here and everything. . . .

EMILY:

Just the same, three years is a long time. Maybe letters from Grover's Corners wouldn't be so interesting after a while. Grover's Corners isn't a very important place when you think of all New Hampshire; but I think it's a very nice town.

GEORGE:

The day wouldn't come when I wouldn't want to know everything that's happening here. I know *that's* true, Emily.

EMILY:

Well, I'll try to make my letters interesting.

> *Pause.*

GEORGE:

Y'know, Emily, whenever I meet a farmer I ask him if he thinks it's important to go to Agriculture School to be a good farmer.

EMILY:

Why, George—

GEORGE:

Yeah, and some of them say that it's even a waste of time. You can get all those things, anyway, out of the pamphlets the government sends out. And Uncle Luke's getting old,—he's about ready for me to start in taking over his farm tomorrow, if I could.

EMILY:

My!

GEORGE:

And, like you say, being gone all that time . . . in other places and meeting other people . . . If anything like that can happen I don't want to go away. I guess new people aren't any better than old ones. I'll bet they almost never are. Emily, . . . I feel that you're as good a friend as I've got. I don't need to go and meet the people in other towns.

EMILY:

But, George, maybe it's very important for you to go and learn all that about cattle-judging and soils and those things. And if you're going into politics, maybe you ought to meet people from other parts of the State . . . of course, I don't know.

GEORGE:

After a pause.

Emily, I'm going to make up my mind right now. I won't go. I'll tell Pa about it tonight.

78

EMILY:

Why, George, I don't see why you have to decide right now. It's a whole year away.

GEORGE:

Emily, I'm glad you spoke to me about that . . . that fault in my character. And what you said was right; but there was *one* thing wrong in it, and that was when you said that for a year I wasn't noticing people, and . . . you, for instance. Listen, Emily . . . you say you were watching me when I did everything. . . . Why, I was doing the same about you all the time. Why, sure,—I always thought about you as one of the chief people I thought about. I always made sure where you were sitting on the bleachers, and who you were with. And we've always had lots of talks . . . and joking, in the halls; and they always meant a lot to me. Of course, they weren't as good as the talk we're having now. Lately I'd been noticing that you'd been acting kind of funny to me, and for three days I've been trying to walk home with you, but something's always got in the way. Yesterday I was standing over against the wall waiting for you, and you walked home with Miss Corcoran.

EMILY:

George! . . . Life's awful funny! How could I have known that? Why, I thought—

GEORGE:

Listen, Emily, I'm going to tell you why I'm not going

79

to Agriculture School. I think that once you've found a person that you've very fond of ... I mean a person who's fond of you, too,—at least enough to be interested in your character ... Well, I think that's just as important as college is, and even more so. That's what I think.

EMILY:

I think it's awfully important, too.

GEORGE:

Emily.

EMILY:

Yes, George.

GEORGE:

Emily, if I improve and make a big change ... would you be ... I mean: *could* you be ...

EMILY:

I ... I am now; I always have been.

GEORGE:

> *Pause.*

So I guess this is an important talk we've been having.

EMILY:

Yes.

GEORGE:

> *Takes a deep breath and straightens his back.*

Wait just a minute and I'll take you home.

> *He rises and goes to the* STAGE MANAGER *who appears and comes toward him.*

Mr. Morgan, I'll have to go home and get the money to pay you for this. It'll only take me a minute.

STAGE MANAGER:

What's that? George Gibbs, do you mean to tell me—!

GEORGE:

Yes, but I had reasons, Mr. Morgan.—Look, here's my gold watch to keep until I come back with the money.

STAGE MANAGER:

That's all right. Keep your watch. I'll trust you.

GEORGE:

I'll be back in five minutes.

STAGE MANAGER:

I'll trust you ten years, George,—not a day more.—Got all over your shock, Emily?

EMILY:

Yes, thank you, Mr. Morgan. It was nothing.

GEORGE:

Taking up the books from the counter.

I'm ready.

They walk in grave silence down the stage, turn, and pass through the trellis at the Webbs' back door and disappear.

STAGE MANAGER:

Thank you, Emily. Thank you, George.
Now before we go on to the wedding, there are still some more things we ought to know about this—about this marriage.

I want to know some more about how the parents took
it; but what I want to know most of all is: oh, you know
what I mean,—what Grover's Corners thought about marriage anyway.

You know's well as I do: people are never able to say right
out what they think of money, or death, or fame, or marriage. You've got to catch it between the lines; you've
got to *over*-hear it.

Oh, Doctor! Mrs. Gibbs!

> *They appear at their side of the stage and
> exchange a glance of understanding with him.
> The* STAGE MANAGER *lays the same plank
> across two chairs that served as a drugstore
> counter and it has now become* MRS. GIBBS'S
> *ironing board.* DR. GIBBS *sits down in a rocker
> and smokes.*
>
> MRS. GIBBS *irons a moment in silence; then
> goes to the foot of the stairs and calls:*

MRS. GIBBS:

Rebecca! It's time you turned out your light and went
to sleep. George, you'd better get some sleep, too.

REBECCA'S VOICE:

Ma, I haven't finished my English.

MRS. GIBBS:

What? Well, I bet you haven't been working, Rebecca.
You've been reading that Sears, Roebuck catalogue, that's
what you've been doing.—All right, I'll give you ten more

minutes. If you haven't finished by then you'll just have to fail the course and be a disgrace to your father and me. —George, what are you doing?

GEORGE'S VOICE:

> *Hurt.*

I'm doing history.

MRS. GIBBS:

Well, you'd better go to bed. You're probably sleeping at the desk as it is.

> *She casts an amused eye at her husband and returns to her ironing.*

DR. GIBBS:

I had a long talk with the boy today.

MRS. GIBBS:

Did you?

DR. GIBBS:

I tell you, Mrs. G., there's nothing so terrifying in the world as a son. The relation of a father to a son is the damnedest, awkwardest—. I always come away feeling like a soggy sponge of hypocrisy.

MRS. GIBBS:

Well, a mother and a daughter's no picnic, let me tell you.

DR. GIBBS:

George is set on it: he wants to marry Emily 'soon as school's out and take her right on to the farm.

> *Pause.*

83

He says he can sit up nights and learn agriculture from government pamphlets, without going to college for it.

MRS. GIBBS:

He always was crazy about farming. Gets that from my people.

DR. GIBBS:

At a pinch, I guess he could start in farming;—but I swear I think he's too young to get married. Julia, he's just a green half-grown kid. He isn't ready to be a family man.

MRS. GIBBS:

No, he ain't. You're right.—But he's a good boy and I wouldn't like to think of him being alone out there ... coming into town Satiddy nights, like any old farm hand, tuckered out from work and looking for excitement. He might get into bad ways. It wouldn't be enough fun for him to come and sit by our stove,—and holding hands with Emily, for a year mightn't be enough either. He might lose interest in her.

DR. GIBBS:

Hm.

MRS. GIBBS:

Frank, I ' been watching her. George is a lucky boy when you think of all the silly girls in the world.

DR. GIBBS:

But, Julia,—George *married*. That great gangling selfish nincumpoop.

84

MRS. GIBBS:

Yes, I know.

She takes up a collar and examines it.

Frank, what do you do to your collars? Do you gnaw 'em? I never saw such a man for collars.

DR. GIBBS:

Julia, when I married you, do you know what one of my terrors was in getting married?

MRS. GIBBS:

Pshaw! Go on with you!

DR. GIBBS:

I was afraid we weren't going to have material for conversation more'n 'ld last us a few weeks. I was afraid we'd run out and eat our meals in silence, that's a fact. You and I've been conversing for twenty years now without any noticeable barren spells.

MRS. GIBBS:

Well, good weather, bad weather, 'tain't very choice, but I always manage to find something to say.

Pause.

DR. GIBBS:

What do you think? What do you think, Julia? Shall we tell the boy he can go ahead and get married?

MRS. GIBBS:

Seems like it's up to us to decide. Myrtle and Charles Webb are willing. They think it's a good idea to throw

85

the young people into the sea and let'm sink or swim, as soon as they're ready.

DR. GIBBS:

What does that mean? Must we decide right now? This minute?

MRS. GIBBS:

There you go putting the responsibility on me!

DR. GIBBS:

Here it is, almost April.—I'll go up and say a word to him right now before he goes to bed.

He rises.

You're sure, Julia? You've nothing more to add?

MRS. GIBBS:

Stops ironing a moment.

I don't know what to say. Seems like it's too much to ask, for a big outdoor boy like that to go and get shut up in classrooms for three years. And once he's on the farm, he might just as well have a companion, seeing he's found a fine girl like Emily.... People are meant to live two by two in this world.... Yes, Frank, go up and tell him it's all right.

DR. GIBBS:

Crosses and is about to call when—

MRS. GIBBS:

Her hands on her cheeks, staring into the audience, in sharp alarm:

Wait a minute! Wait a minute!—

86

Then resuming her ironing.

No,—go and tell him.

DR. GIBBS:

Why did you stop then, Julia?

MRS. GIBBS:

Oh, you know: I thought of all those times we went
through in the first years when George and Rebecca were
babies,—you walking up and down with them at three
in the morning; the whooping-cough; the time George
fell off the porch. You and I were twenty-five years old,
and more. It's wonderful how one forgets one's troubles,
like that.—Yes, Frank, go upstairs and tell him.... It's
worth it.

DR. GIBBS:

Yes, they'll have a lot of troubles, but that's none of our
business. Let'm. Everybody has a right to his own troubles.
—You ought to be present, Julia,—important occasion like
that. I'll call him.—George! Oh, George!

GEORGE'S VOICE:

Yes, Pa.

DR. GIBBS:

Can you come down a minute? Your mother and I want
to speak to you.

GEORGE:

Yeah, sure.

MRS. GIBBS:

Putting her arm through her husband's.

Lord, what a fool I am: I'm trembling all over. There's nothing to tremble about.

STAGE MANAGER:

Thank you! Thank you!

Now we're ready to go on with the wedding.

> *While he talks, the actors remove the chair and tables and trellises from the Gibbs and Webb homes.*
>
> *They arrange the pews for the church in the back of the stage. The congregation will sit facing the back wall. The aisle of the church is in the middle of the scene.*
>
> *A small platform is placed against the back wall on which the* STAGE MANAGER *as Minister can stand.*

There are a lot of things to be said about a wedding; there are a lot of thoughts that go on during a wedding.

We can't get them all into one wedding, ~~naturally, and~~ especially not into a wedding at Grover's Corners where they're awfully plain and short.

In this ~~wedding~~ I ~~play~~ the minister. That gives me the right to say a few more things about it.

For a while now, the play gets pretty serious.

Y'see, some churches say that marriage is a sacrament. I don't quite know what that means, but I can guess. Like Mrs. Gibbs said a few minutes ago: People were made to live two-by-two.

88

[handwritten: the people are pretty young]

This is a good wedding, but people are so put together
that even at a good wedding there's a lot of confusion
way down deep in people's minds and we thought that
that ought to be in our play, too.

[handwritten: but they come from good stock and they chose right]

The real hero of this scene isn't on the stage at all, and *[handwritten: I guess]*
you know who that is. It's like what one of those Euro-
pean fellas said: every child born into the world is Nature's attempt to make a perfect human being. Well,
we've seen nature pushing and contriving for some time
now. We all know that nature's interested in quantity;
but I think she's interested in quality, too,—that's why
I'm in the ministry.—Maybe she's trying to make another
good governor for New Hampshire. — *[handwritten: That is what Emily hopes]*
And don't forget the other witnesses at this wedding,—
the ancestors. Millions of them. Most of them set out to
live two-by-two, also. Millions of them.

Well, that's all my sermon. 'Twan't very long, anyway.

> *The organ starts playing Handel's "Largo."*
> *The congregation streams into the church and*
> *sits in silence.*
>
> MRS. WEBB, *on the way to her place, turns*
> *back and speaks to the audience.*

MRS. WEBB:

I don't know why on earth I should be crying. I suppose
there's nothing to cry about. It came over me at breakfast this morning; there was Emily eating her breakfast

as she's done for seventeen years and now she's going off to eat it in someone else's house. I suppose that's it.

And Emily! She suddenly said: I can't eat another mouthful, and she put her head down on the table and *she* cried.

> *She starts toward her seat in the church, but turns back and adds:*

Oh, I've got to say it: you know, there's something downright cruel about sending our girls out into marriage this way.

I hope some of her girl friends have told her a thing or two. It's cruel, I know, but I couldn't bring myself to say anything. I went into it blind as a bat myself.

The whole world's wrong, that's what's the matter.

There they come.

> *She hurries to her place in the pew.*
>
> GEORGE *starts to come down the right aisle of the theater, through the audience.*
>
> *Suddenly three members of his baseball team appear by the right proscenium pillar and start whistling and catcalling to him. They are dressed for the ball field.*

THE BASEBALL PLAYERS:

Eh, George, George! Hsst—yaow! If things don't go right, call us in. We know what to do. Eh, fellas? Yaow! George, don't look so innocent, you old geezer. We know what you're thinking. Don't disgrace the team, big boy. Whoo-oo-oo.

STAGE MANAGER:

All right! All right! That'll do. That's enough of that.

> *Smiling, he pushes them off the stage. They lean back to shout a few more catcalls.*

There used to be an awful lot of that kind of thing at weddings in the old days,—Rome, and later. We're more civilized now,—so they say.

> *The choir starts singing "Love divine, all love excelling—." George has reached the stage. He stares at the congregation a moment, then takes a few steps of withdrawal, toward the right proscenium pillar.*

GEORGE:

> *Darkly, to himself.*

I wish I were back at school. . . . I don't want to get married.

> *His mother has left her seat and come toward him. She stops, looking at him anxiously.*

MRS. GIBBS:

George, what's the matter?

GEORGE:

Ma, I don't want to grow *old*. Why's everybody pushing me so?

MRS. GIBBS:

Why, George . . . you wanted it.

GEORGE:

Why do I have to get married at all? Listen, Ma, for the last time I ask you—

MRS. GIBBS:

No, no, George ... you're a man now.

GEORGE:

Listen, Ma, you never listen to me. All I want to do is to be a fella ... why do—

MRS. GIBBS:

George! If anyone should hear you! Now stop. Why, I'm ashamed of you!

GEORGE:

Passing his hand over his forehead.

What's the matter? I've been dreaming. Where's Emily?

MRS. GIBBS:

Gracious! You gave me such a turn.

GEORGE:

Cheer up, Ma. What are you looking so funny for? Cheer up; I'm getting married.

MRS. GIBBS:

Let me catch my breath a minute.

GEORGE:

Now, Ma, you save Thursday nights. Emily and I are coming over to dinner every Thursday night ... you'll see. Ma, what are you crying for? Come on; we've got to get ready for this.

In the meantime, EMILY, *in white and wearing*

*her wedding veil, has come through the audi-
ence and mounted on to the stage. She too
draws back when she sees the congregation in
the church. The choir begins: "Blessed be the
tie that binds."*

EMILY:

I never felt so alone in my whole life. And George over
there, looking so...! I *hate* him. I wish I were dead.
Papa! Papa!

MR. WEBB:

*Leaves his seat in the pews and comes toward
her anxiously.*

Emily! Emily! Now don't get upset....

EMILY:

But, Papa,—I don't want to get married....

MR. WEBB:

Sh-sh— Emily. Everything's all right.

EMILY:

Why can't I stay for a while just as I am? Let's go away.

MR. WEBB:

No, no, Emily. Now stop and think.

EMILY:

Don't you remember that you used to say,—all the time
you used to say that I was *your* girl. There must be lots
of places we can go to. Let's go away. I'll work for you.
I could keep house.

MR. WEBB:

Sh.... You mustn't think of such things. You're just nervous, Emily. Now, now,—you're marrying the best young fellow in the world. George is a fine fellow.

EMILY:

But, Papa,—

MR. WEBB:

George! George!

>   MRS. GIBBS *returns to her seat.*
>
>   GEORGE *hears* MR. WEBB *and looks up.*
>
>   MR. WEBB *beckons to him. They move to the center of the stage.*

I'm giving away my daughter, George. Do you think you can take care of her?

GEORGE:

Mr. Webb, I want to . . . I want to try. Emily, I'm going to do my best. I love you, Emily. I need you.

EMILY:

Well, if you love me, help me. All I want is someone to love me.

GEORGE:

I will, Emily.

EMILY:

If ever I'm sick or in trouble, that's what I mean.

GEORGE:

Emily, I'll try. I'll try.

94

EMILY:

And I mean for *ever*. Do you hear? For ever and ever.

They fall into each other's arms.

The March from "Lohengrin" is heard.

MR. WEBB:

Come, they're waiting for us. Now you know it'll be all right. Come, quick.

GEORGE *slips away and takes his place beside the* STAGE MANAGER-CLERGYMAN.

EMILY *proceeds up the aisle on her father's arm.*

STAGE MANAGER:

Do you, George, take this woman, Emily, to be your wedded wife, to have . . .

MRS. SOAMES *has been sitting in the last row of the congregation.*

She now turns to her neighbors and in a shrill voice says:

MRS. SOAMES:

Perfectly lovely wedding! Loveliest wedding I ever saw. Oh, I do love a good wedding, don't you? Doesn't she make a lovely bride?

GEORGE:

I do.

STAGE MANAGER:

Do you, Emily, take this man, George, to be your wedded husband,—

MRS. SOAMES:

Don't know *when* I've seen such a lovely wedding. But I always cry. Don't know why it is, but I always cry. I just like to see young people happy, don't you? Oh, I think it's lovely.

> *The ring.*
> *The kiss.*
> *The stage is suddenly arrested into silent tableau.*
> *The* STAGE MANAGER, *his eyes on the distance, says to the audience:*

I've married two hundred couples in my day.
Do I believe in it?
I don't know.
M.... marries N.... millions of them.
The cottage, the gocart, the Sunday afternoon drives in the Ford, the first rheumatism, the grandchildren, the second rheumatism, the deathbed, the reading of the will,—
Once in a thousand times it's interesting.
Well, let's have Mendelssohn's "Wedding March"!

> *The organ picks up the March.*
> *The bride and groom come down the aisle, radiant, but trying to be very dignified.*

MRS. SOAMES:

Aren't they a lovely couple? Oh, I've never been to such a nice wedding. I'm sure they'll be happy. I always say:

96

happiness, that's the great thing! The important thing is to be happy.

> *The bride and groom reach the steps leading into the audience. A bright light is thrown upon them. They descend into the auditorium and run up the aisle joyously.*

STAGE MANAGER:

That's all the Second Act. Ten minutes' intermission, folks.

ACT THREE

*During the intermission the audience has seen
the actors arranging the stage. On the right
hand side, a little right of the center, ten or
twelve ordinary chairs have been placed in
three openly spaced rows facing the audience.
These are graves in the cemetery.*

*Towards the end of the intermission the actors
enter and take their places. The front row
contains: toward the center of the stage, an
empty chair; then* MRS. GIBBS; SIMON STIMSON.
The second row contains, among others, MRS.
SOAMES. *The third row has* WALLY WEBB.

*The dead sit in a quiet without stiffness, and
in a patience without listlessness.*

The STAGE MANAGER *takes his accustomed place
and waits for the house-lights to go down.*

STAGE MANAGER:

This time nine years have gone by, friends—summer, 1913.
Gradual changes in Grover's Corners. Horses are getting
rarer. Farmers coming into town in Fords.
Chief difference is in the young people, far as I can see.
They want to go to the moving pictures all the time.

98

They want to wear clothes like they see there ... want
to be citified.

Everybody locks their house doors now at night. Ain't
been any burglars in town yet, but everybody's heard
about 'em.

But you'd be surprised though—on the whole, things
don't change much at Grover's Corners.
Guess you want to know what all these chairs are here
fur. Smarter ones have guessed it already. I don't know
how you feel about such things; but this certainly is a
beautiful place. It's on a hillhop—a windy hilltop—lots of
sky, lots of clouds,—often lots of sun and moon and stars.
You come up here on a fine afternoon and you can see
range on range of hills—awful blue they are—up there by
Lake Sunapee and Lake Winnapassaukee ... and way up, ·
if you've got a glass, you can see the White Mountains
and Mt. Washington—where North Conway and Conway
is. And, of course, our favorite mountain, Mt. Monad-
nock's, right here—and all around it lie these towns—
Jaffrey, 'n East Jaffrey, 'n Peterborough, 'n Dublin and

Then pointing down in the audience.

there, quite a ways down is Grover's Corners.
Yes, beautiful spot up here. Mountain laurel and li-lacks.
I often wonder why people like to be buried in Wood-
lawn and Brooklyn when they might pass the same time
up here in New Hampshire.

99

OUR TOWN

Over in _her_ corner—

Pointing to stage left.

are the old stones,—1670, 1680. Strong-minded people
that come a long way to be independent. Summer people
walk around there laughing at the funny words on the
tombstones . . . it don't do any harm. And genealogists
come up from Boston—get paid by city people for looking up their ancestors. They want to make sure they're
Daughters of the American Revolution and of the _May-
flower_. . . . Well, I guess that don't do any harm, either.
Wherever you come near the human race, there's layers
and layers of nonsense. . . .

Over there are some Civil War veterans too. Iron flags
on their graves. . . . New Hampshire boys . . . had a notion
that the Union ought to be kept together, though they'd
never seen more than fifty miles of it themselves. All they
knew was the name, friends—the United States of America. The United States of America. And they went and
died about it.

This here is the new part of the cemetery. Here's your
friend, Mrs. Gibbs. 'N let me see— _and_ Here's Mr. Stimson,
organist at the Congregational Church. And over there's
Mrs. Soames who enjoyed the wedding so—you remember? Oh, and a lot of others. And Editor Webb's boy,
Wallace, whose appendix burst while he was on a Boy
Scout trip to Crawford Notch.

100

Yes, an awful lot of sorrow has sort of quieted down up
here. People just wild with grief have brought their rela-
tives up to this hill. We all know how it is ... and then *we all know*
time ... and sunny days ... and rainy days ... 'n snow. ... *how it is*
tz-tz-tz. We're all glad they're in a beautiful place and
we're coming up here ourselves when our fit's over.
This certainly is an important part of Grover's Corners.
A lot of thoughts come up here, night and day, but
there's no post office. *they are*
Now I'm going to tell you some things you know al- *we all know*
ready. You know'm as well as I do; but you don't take'm
out and look at'm very often. *we all know that*
I don't care what they say with their mouths—everybody
knows that *something* is eternal. And it ain't houses and it
ain't names, and it ain't earth, and it ain't even the stars ...
everybody knows in their bones that *something* is eternal,
and that something has to do with human beings. All the
greatest people ever lived have been telling us that for
five thousand years and yet you'd be surprised how people are always losing hold of it. There's something way
down deep that's eternal about every human being.

Pause.

You know as well as I do that the dead don't stay interested in us living people for very long. Gradually, gradually, they let hold of the earth ... and the ambitions they
had ... and the pleasures they had ... and the things they
suffered ... and the people they loved.

They get weaned away from earth—that's the way I put it,—weaned away.

Yes, they stay here while the earth-part of 'em burns away, burns out, and all that time they slowly get indifferent to what's goin' on in Grover's Corners.

They're waitin'. They're waitin' for something that they feel is comin'. Something important and great. Aren't they waitin' for the eternal part in them to come out clear?

Some of the things they're going to say maybe'll hurt your feelings—but that's the way it is: mother'n daughter ... husband 'n wife ... enemy n' enemy ... money 'n miser ... all those terribly important things kind of grow pale around here. And what's left? What's left when memory's gone, and your identity, Mrs. Smith?

> *He looks at the audience a minute, then turns to the stage.*

Well! There are some *living* people. There's Joe Stoddard, our undertaker, supervising a new-made grave. And here comes a Grover's Corners boy, that left town to go out West.

> JOE STODDARD *has hovered about in the background.* SAM CRAIG *enters left, wiping his forehead from the exertion. He carries an umbrella and strolls front.*

SAM CRAIG:

Good afternoon, Joe Stoddard.

JOE STODDARD:

Good afternoon, good afternoon. Let me see now: do I know you?

SAM CRAIG:

I'm Sam Craig.

JOE STODDARD:

Gracious sakes' alive! Of all people! I should'a knowed you'd be back for the funeral. You've been away a long time, Sam.

SAM CRAIG:

Yes, I've been away over twelve years. I'm in business out in Buffalo now, Joe. But I was in the East when I got news of my cousin's death, so I thought I'd combine things a little and come and see the old home. You look well.

JOE STODDARD:

Yes, yes, can't complain. Very sad, our journey today, Samuel.

SAM CRAIG:

Yes.

JOE STODDARD:

Yes, yes. I always say, I hate to supervise when a young person is taken. I see you brought your umbrella. It's going to rain and make it sadder still, seems like. They'll be here in a few minutes now. I had to come here early today—my son's supervisin' at the home.

OUR TOWN

SAM CRAIG:

Reading stones.

Old Farmer McCarty, I used to do chores for him—after school. He had the lumbago.

JOE STODDARD:

Yes, we brought Farmer McCarty here a number of years ago now.

SAM CRAIG:

Staring at MRS. GIBBS' *knees.*

Why, this is my Aunt Julia.... I'd forgotten that she'd ...of course, of course.

JOE STODDARD:

Yes, Doc Gibbs lost his wife two-three years ago... about this time. And today's another ~~pretty~~ bad blow for him, too.

MRS. GIBBS:

To SIMON STIMSON: *in an even voice.*

That's my sister Carey's boy, Sam.... Sam Craig.

SIMON STIMSON:

I'm always uncomfortable when *they're* around.

MRS. GIBBS:

Simon.

SIMON STIMSON:

~~They and their nonsense and their damned glee at being alive....~~

MRS. GIBBS:

Simon, be patient....

104

SAM CRAIG:

Do they choose their own verses much, Joe?

JOE STODDARD:

No... not usual. Mostly the bereaved pick a verse.

SAM CRAIG:

Doesn't sound like Aunt Julia. There aren't many of those Hersey sisters left now. Let me see: where are... I wanted to look at my father's and mother's...

JOE STODDARD:

Over there with the Craigs.... Avenue F.

SAM CRAIG:

Reading SIMON STIMSON's *epitaph.*

He was organist at church, wasn't he?—Hm, drank a lot, we used to say.

JOE STODDARD:

Nobody was supposed to know about it. He'd seen a peck of trouble. Those musical fellas ain't like the rest of us, I reckon.

Behind his hand.

Took his own life, y' know?

SAM CRAIG:

Oh, did he?

JOE STODDARD:

Hung himself in the attic. They tried to hush it up, but of course it got around. His wife's just married Senator Barstow. Many a time I've seen her, eleven o'clock at

105

night, goin' around the streets huntin' for her husband.
Think o' that! Now she's married to Senator Barstow
over at Manchester. He chose his own epy-taph. You can
see it there. It ain't a verse exactly.

SAM CRAIG:

Why, it's just some notes of music—what is it?

JOE STODDARD:

Oh, I wouldn't know. It was wrote up in the Boston
papers at the time.

SAM CRAIG:

Joe, what did she die of?

JOE STODDARD:

Who?

SAM CRAIG:

My cousin.

JOE STODDARD:

Oh, didn't you know? Had some trouble bringing a baby
into the world. Let's see, today's Friday—'twas almost a
week ago now.

SAM CRAIG:

Putting up his umbrella.

Did the baby live?

JOE STODDARD:

Raising his coat collar.

No. 'Twas her second, though. There's a little boy 'bout
four years old.

106

SAM CRAIG:

The grave's going to be over there?

JOE STODDARD:

Yes, there ain't much more room over here among the Gibbses, so they're opening up a whole new Gibbs section over by Avenue B. You'll excuse me now. I see they're comin'.

THE DEAD:

Not lugubrious; and strongly New England in accent.

Rain'll do a lot of good.—Yes, reckon things were gettin' downright parched. Don't look like it's goin' to last long, tho'.—Lemuel, you remember the floods of '79? Carried away all the bridges but one.

From left to right, at the back of the stage, comes a procession. Four men carry a casket, invisible to us. All the rest are under umbrellas. One can vaguely see: DR. GIBBS, GEORGE, *the* WEBBS, *etc. They gather about a grave in the back center of the stage, a little to the left of center.*

MRS. SOAMES:

Who is it, Julia?

MRS. GIBBS:

Without raising her eyes.

My daughter-in-law, Emily Webb.

107

MRS. SOAMES:

> *A little surprised, but no emotion.*

Well, I declare! The road up here must have been awful muddy. What did she die of, Julia?

MRS. GIBBS:

In childbirth.

MRS. SOAMES:

Childbirth.

> *Almost with a laugh.*

I'd forgotten all about that! My, wasn't life awful—

> *With a sigh.*

and wonderful.

SIMON STIMSON:

> *With a sideways glance.*

Wonderful, was it?

MRS. GIBBS:

Simon! Now, remember!

MRS. SOAMES:

I remember Emily's wedding. Wasn't it a lovely wedding! And I remember her reading the class poem at Graduation Exercises. Emily was one of the brightest girls ever graduated from High School. I've heard Principal Wilkins say so time after time. I called on them at their new farm, just before I died. Perfectly beautiful farm.

A WOMAN FROM AMONG THE DEAD:

It's on the same road we lived on.

108

A MAN AMONG THE DEAD:

Yes, just near the Elks' picnic grounds. Remember, Joe? By the lake where we always used to go Fourth of July? Right smart farm.

> *They subside. The group by the grave starts singing "Blessed be the tie that binds."*

A WOMAN AMONG THE DEAD:

I always liked that hymn. I was hopin' they'd sing a hymn.

A MAN AMONG THE DEAD:

My wife—my second wife—knows all the verses of about every hymn there is. It just beats the Dutch . . . she can go through them all by heart.

> *Pause. Suddenly* EMILY *appears from among the umbrellas. She is wearing a white dress. Her hair is down her back and tied by a white ribbon like a little girl. She comes slowly, gazing wonderingly at the dead, a little dazed. She stops halfway and smiles faintly.*

EMILY:

Hello.

VOICES AMONG THE DEAD:

Hello, Emily. H'lo, M's. Gibbs.

EMILY:

Hello, Mother Gibbs.

MRS. GIBBS:

Emily.

EMILY:

Hello.

The hymn continues. EMILY *looks back at the funeral. She says dreamily:*

It's raining.

MRS. GIBBS:

Yes. . . . They'll be gone soon, dear. Just rest yourself.

EMILY *sits down in the empty chair by* MRS. GIBBS.

EMILY:

It seems thousands and thousands of years since I. . . . How stupid they all look. They don't have to look like that!

MRS. GIBBS:

Don't look at them now, dear. They'll be gone soon.

EMILY:

Oh, I wish I'd been here a long time. I don't like being new here.—How do you do, Mr. Stimson?

SIMON STIMSON:

How do you do, Emily.

EMILY *continues to look about her with a wan and wondering smile; but for a moment her eyes do not return to the funeral group. As though to shut out from her mind the thought of that group she starts speaking to* MRS. GIBBS *with a touch of nervousness.*

EMILY:

Mother Gibbs, George and I have made that farm into

just the best place you ever saw. We thought of you all the time. We wanted to show you the new barn and a great long ce-ment drinking fountain for the stock. We bought that out of the money you left us.

MRS. GIBBS:

I did?

EMILY:

Don't you remember, Mother Gibbs—the legacy you left us? Why, it was over three hundred and fifty dollars.

MRS. GIBBS:

Yes, yes, Emily.

EMILY:

Well, there's a patent device on this drinking fountain so that it never overflows, Mother Gibbs, and it never sinks below a certain mark they have there. It's fine.

> Her voice trails off and her eyes return to the funeral group.

It won't be the same to George without me, but it's a lovely farm.

> Suddenly she looks directly at MRS. GIBBS.

Live people don't understand, do they?

MRS. GIBBS:

No, dear—not very much.

EMILY:

They're sort of shut up in little boxes, aren't they? I feel as though I knew them last a thousand years ago.... My boy is spending the day at Mrs. Carter's.

She sees MR. CARTER *among the dead.*

Oh, Mr. Carter, my little boy is spending the day at your house.

MR. CARTER:

Is he?

EMILY:

Yes, he loves it there.—Mother Gibbs, we have a Ford, too. Never gives any trouble. I don't drive, though. Mother Gibbs, when does this feeling go away?—Of being ... one of *them?* How long does it ...?

MRS. GIBBS:

Sh! dear. Just wait and be patient.

EMILY:

With a sigh.

I know.—Look, they're finished. They're going.

MRS. GIBBS:

Sh—.

The umbrellas leave the stage. DR. GIBBS *comes over to his wife's grave and stands before it a moment.* EMILY *looks up at his face.* MRS. GIBBS *does not raise her eyes.*

EMILY:

Look! Father Gibbs is bringing some of my flowers to you. He looks just like George, doesn't he? Oh, Mother Gibbs, I never realized before how troubled and how ... how in the dark live persons are. From morning till night, that's all they are—troubled.

DR. GIBBS *goes off.*

THE DEAD:

Little cooler than it was.—Yes, that rain's cooled it off a little. Those North East winds always do the same thing, don't they? If it isn't a rain, it's a three-day blow.— Reckon it may clear up before night; often does.

> *A patient calm falls on the stage. The* STAGE MANAGER *appears at his proscenium pillar, smoking.* EMILY *sits up abruptly with an idea.*

EMILY:

But, Mother Gibbs, one can go back; one can go back there again ... into living. I feel it. I know it. Why just then for a moment I was thinking about ... about the farm ... and for a minute I *was* there, and my baby was on my lap as plain as day.

MRS. GIBBS:

Yes, of course you can.

EMILY:

I can go back there and live all those days over again ... why not?

MRS. GIBBS:

All I can say is, Emily, don't.

EMILY:

> *Takes a few steps toward the* STAGE MANAGER.

But it's true, isn't it? I can go and live ... back there ... again.

STAGE MANAGER:

Yes, some have tried—but they soon come back here.

113

MRS. GIBBS:

Don't do it, Emily.

MRS. SOAMES:

Emily, don't. It's not what you think it'd be.

EMILY:

But I won't live over a sad day. I'll choose a happy one—
I'll choose the day I first knew that I loved George. Why
should that be painful?

> *They are silent. Her question turns to the*
> STAGE MANAGER.

STAGE MANAGER:

You not only live it; but you watch yourself living it.

EMILY:

Yes?

STAGE MANAGER:

And as you watch it, you see the thing that they—down
there—never know. You see the future. You know what's
going to happen afterwards.

EMILY:

But is that—painful? Why?

MRS. GIBBS:

That's not the only reason why you shouldn't do it,
Emily. When you've been here longer you'll see that our
life here is our hope that soon we'll forget all that, and
think only of what's ahead, and be ready for what's ahead.
When you've been here longer you'll understand.

114

EMILY:

> *Softly.*

But, Mother Gibbs, how can I ever forget that life? It's all I know. It's all I had.

> MRS. GIBBS *does not answer.*

Mr. Stimson, did you go back?

SIMON STIMSON:

> *Sharply.*

No.

EMILY:

Did you, Mrs. Soames?

MRS. SOAMES:

Oh, Emily. It isn't wise. Really, it isn't. All we can do is just warn you. It won't be what you expect.

EMILY:

> *Slowly.*

But it's a thing I must know for myself. I'll choose a happy day, anyway.

MRS. GIBBS:

No. At least, choose an unimportant day. Choose the least important day in your life. It will be important enough.

EMILY:

> *To the* STAGE MANAGER.

Then it can't be since I was married; or since the baby was born. I can choose a birthday at least, can't I?—I choose my twelfth birthday.

OUR TOWN

STAGE MANAGER:

All right. February 11th, 1899. A Tuesday.—Do you want any special time of day?

EMILY:

Oh, I want the whole day.

STAGE MANAGER:

We'll begin at dawn. You remember it had been snowing for several days; but it had stopped the night before, and they had begun clearing the roads. The sun's coming up.

EMILY:

With a cry.

There's Main Street ... why, that's Mr. Morgan's drugstore before he changed it! ... And there's the livery stable.

She walks toward the back of the stage.

STAGE MANAGER:

Yes, it's 1899. This is fourteen years ago.

EMILY:

Oh, that's the town I knew as a little girl. And, look, there's the old white fence that used to be around our house. Oh, I'd forgotten that! Oh, I love it so! Are *they* inside?

STAGE MANAGER:

Yes, your mother'll be coming downstairs in a minute to make breakfast.

EMILY:

Softly.

Will she?

116

STAGE MANAGER:

And you remember: your father had been away for several days; he came back on the early morning train.

EMILY:

No...?

STAGE MANAGER:

He'd been back to his college to make a speech—in Western New York, at Clinton.

EMILY:

Look! There's Howie Newsome. There's our policeman. But he's *dead;* he *died.*

> *The* STAGE MANAGER *retires to his corner. The voices of* HOWIE NEWSOME, CONSTABLE WARREN *and* JOE CROWELL, JR., *are heard at the left of the stage.*

HOWIE NEWSOME:

Whoa, Bessie!—Bessie! 'Morning, Bill.

BILL:

Morning, Howie.

HOWIE NEWSOME:

You're up early.

BILL:

Been rescuin' a party; darn near froze to death, down by Polish Town thar. Got drunk and lay out in the snowdrifts. Thought he was in bed when I shook'm.

EMILY:

Why, there's Joe Crowell....

JOE CROWELL:

Good morning, Mr. Warren. 'Morning, Howie.

> MRS. WEBB *has appeared in her kitchen, but*
> EMILY *does not see her until she calls.*

MRS. WEBB:

Chil-*dren!* Wally! Emily! . . . Time to get up.

EMILY:

Mama, here I am! Oh! how young Mama looks! I didn't
know Mama was ever that young. Oh!

MRS. WEBB:

You can come and dress by the kitchen fire, if you like;
but hurry.

> HOWIE NEWSOME *has entered along Main Street*
> *and brings the milk to* MRS. WEBB's *door.*

Good morning, Mr. Newsome. Whhhh—it's cold.

HOWIE NEWSOME:

Ten below by my barn, Mrs. Webb.

MRS. WEBB:

Think of it! Keep yourself wrapped up.

> *She takes her bottles in, shuddering.*

EMILY:

> *With an effort.*

Mama, I can't find my blue hair ribbon anywhere.

MRS. WEBB:

ENTER Warren

Just open your eyes, dear, that's all. I laid it out for you
special—on the dresser, there. If it were a snake it would
bite you.

118

EMILY:

Yes, yes. . . .

> *She puts her hand on her heart.* MR. WEBB
> *comes along Main Street, where he meets*
> CONSTABLE WARREN.

MR. WEBB:

Good morning, Bill.

BILL:

Good morning, Mr. Webb. You're up early.

MR. WEBB:

Yes, just been back to my old college in New York State.
Been any trouble here?

BILL:

Well, I was called up this mornin' to rescue a Polish fella—
darn near froze to death he was.

MR. WEBB:

We must get it in the paper.

BILL:

'Twan't much.

EMILY:

> *Whispers.*

Papa.

> MR. WEBB *shakes the snow off his feet and*
> *enters his house.*

MR. WEBB:

Good morning, Mother.

MRS. WEBB:

How did it go, Charles?

MR. WEBB:

Oh, fine, I guess. I told'm a few things.

MRS. WEBB:

Did you sit up on the train all night?

MR. WEBB:

Yes. Never could sleep on a Pullman anyway.

MRS. WEBB:

Charles, seems to me—we're rich enough so that you could sleep in a train once in a while.

MR. WEBB:

Everything all right here?

MRS. WEBB:

Yes—can't think of anything that's happened, special. Been right cold. Howie Newsome says it's ten below over to his barn.

MR. WEBB:

Yes, well, it's colder than that at Hamilton College. Students' ears are falling off. It ain't Christian.—Paper have any mistakes in it?

MRS. WEBB:

None that I noticed. Coffee's ready when you want it.

He starts upstairs.

Charles! Don't forget; it's Emily's birthday. Did you remember to get her something?

MR. WEBB:

Patting his pocket.

Yes, I've got something here.

120

MRS. WEBB:

Goodness sakes! I hope she likes what I got for her. I hunted hard enough for it. Child*ren!* Hurry up! Hurry up!

MR. WEBB:

Where's my girl? Where's my birthday girl?

He goes off left.

MRS. WEBB:

Don't interrupt her now, Charles. You can see her at breakfast. She's slow enough as it is. Hurry up, children! It's seven o'clock. Now, I don't want to call you again.

EMILY:

Softly, more in wonder than in grief.

I can't bear it. They're so young and beautiful. Why did they ever have to get old? Mama, I'm here. I'm grown up. I love you all, everything.—I can't look at everything hard enough. There's the butternut tree.

She wanders up Main Street.

There's Mr. Morgan's drugstore. And there's the High School, forever and ever, and ever. And there's the Congregational Church where I got married. Oh, dear. Oh, dear. Oh, dear!

The STAGE MANAGER *beckons partially to her. He points to the house. She says a breathless "yes" and goes to the house.*

Good morning, Mama.

MRS. WEBB:

> *At the foot of the stairs, kissing her in a matter-of-fact way.*

Well, now, dear, a very happy birthday to my girl and many happy returns. There are some surprises waiting for you on the kitchen table.

EMILY:

Oh, Mama, you *shouldn't* have.

> *She throws an anguished glance at the* STAGE MANAGER.

I can't—I can't.

MRS. WEBB:

> *Facing the audience, over her stove.*

But birthday or no birthday, I want you to eat your breakfast good and slow. I want you to grow up and be a good strong girl.

> *She goes to the stairs and calls.*

Wally! Wally, wash yourself good. Everything's getting cold down here.

> *She returns to the stove with her back to* EMILY. EMILY *opens her parcels.*

That in the blue paper is from your Aunt Carrie and I reckon you can guess who brought the post card album. I found it on the doorstep when I brought in the milk— George Gibbs . . . must have come over in the cold pretty early . . . right nice of him.

EMILY:

> *To herself.*

Oh, George! I'd forgotten that....

MRS. WEBB:

Chew that bacon slow. It'll help keep you warm on a cold day.

EMILY:

> *Beginning softly but urgently.*

Oh, Mama, just look at me one minute as though you really saw me. Mama, fourteen years have gone by. I'm dead. You're a grandmother, Mama. I married George Gibbs, Mama. Wally's dead, too. Mama, his appendix burst on a camping trip to North Conway. We felt just terrible about it—don't you remember? But, just for a moment now we're all together. Mama, just for a moment we're happy. Let's look at one another.

MRS. WEBB:

That in the yellow paper is something I found in the attic among your grandmother's things. You're old enough to wear it now, and I thought you'd like it.

EMILY:

And this is from you. Why, Mama, it's just lovely and it's just what I wanted. It's beautiful!

> *She flings her arms around her mother's neck.*
> *Her mother goes on with her cooking, but is*
> *pleased.*

MRS. WEBB:

Well, I hoped you'd like it. Hunted all over. Your Aunt Norah couldn't find one in Concord, so I had to send all the way to Boston.

Laughing.

Wally has something for you, too. He made it at Manual Training class and he's very proud of it. Be sure you make a big fuss about it.—Your father has a surprise for you, too; don't know what it is myself. Sh—here he comes.

MR. WEBB:

Off stage.

Where's my girl? Where's my birthday girl?

EMILY:

In a loud voice to the STAGE MANAGER.

I can't. I can't go on. Oh! Oh. It goes so fast. We don't have time to look at one another.

She breaks down sobbing. At a gesture from the STAGE MANAGER, MRS. WEBB *disappears.*

I didn't realize. So all that was going on and we never noticed. Take me back—up the hill—to my grave. But first: Wait! One more look. Good-by, Good-by, world. Good-by, Grover's Corners . . . Mama and Papa. Good-by to clocks ticking . . . and Mama's sunflowers. And food and coffee. And new-ironed dresses and hot baths . . . and sleeping and waking up. Oh, earth, you're too wonderful for anybody to realize you.

She looks toward the STAGE MANAGER *and asks*
abruptly, through her tears.

Do any human beings ever realize life while they live it?—
every, every minute?

STAGE MANAGER:

No.

Pause.

The saints and poets, maybe—they do some.

EMILY:

I'm ready to go back.

She returns to her chair beside MRS. GIBBS.

Mother Gibbs, I should have listened to you. Now I want
to be quiet for a while.—Oh, Mother Gibbs, I saw it all.
I saw your garden.

MRS. GIBBS:

Did you, dear?

EMILY:

That's all human beings are!—Just blind people.

MRS. GIBBS:

Look, it's clearing up. The stars are coming out.

EMILY:

Oh, Mr. Stimson, I should have listened to them.

SIMON STIMSON:

With mounting violence; bitingly.

Yes, now you know. Now you know! That's what it was
to be alive. To move about in a cloud of ignorance; to go
up and down trampling on the feelings of those . . . of

125

those about you. To spend and waste time as though you had a million years. To be always at the mercy of one self-centered passion, or another. Now you know—that's the happy existence you wanted to go back and see. Did you shout to 'em? Did you call to 'em?

EMILY:

Yes, I did.

SIMON STIMSON:

Now you know them as they are: in ignorance and blindness.

MRS. GIBBS:

Spiritedly.

Simon Stimson, that ain't the whole truth and you know it.

The dead have begun to stir.

THE DEAD:

Lemuel, wind's coming up, seems like.—Oh, dear,—I keep remembering things tonight.—It's right cold for June, ain't it?

MRS. GIBBS:

Look what you've done, you and your rebellious spirit stirring us up here.—Emily, look at that star. I forget its name.

THE DEAD:

I'm getting to know them all, but I don't know their names.—My boy Joel was a sailor,—knew 'em all. He'd set on the porch evenings and tell 'em all by name. Yes, sir,

126

it was wonderful.—A star's mighty good company.—Yes, yes.—Yes, 'tis.

SIMON STIMSON:

Here's one of *them* coming.

THE DEAD:

That's funny. 'Taint no time for one of them to be here. —Goodness sakes.

EMILY:

Mother Gibbs, it's George.

MRS. GIBBS:

Sh, dear. You just rest yourself.

EMILY:

It's George.

> GEORGE *enters from the left, and slowly comes toward them.*

A MAN FROM AMONG THE DEAD:

And my boy, Joel, who knew the stars—he used to say it took millions of years for that speck o' light to git to the earth. Don't seem like a body could believe it, but that's what he used to say—millions of years.

ANOTHER:

That's what they say.

> GEORGE *flings himself on* EMILY's *grave.*

THE DEAD:

Goodness! That ain't no way to behave!—He ought to be home.

EMILY:

Mother Gibbs?

MRS. GIBBS:

Yes, Emily?

EMILY:

They don't understand much, do they?

MRS. GIBBS:

No, dear, not very much. *they dont understand*

> *The* STAGE MANAGER *appears at the right, one hand on a dark curtain which he slowly draws across the scene.*
>
> *In the distance a clock is heard striking the hour very faintly.*

STAGE MANAGER:

Most everybody's asleep in Grover's Corners. There are a few lights on: Shorty Hawkins, down at the depot, has just watched the Albany train go by. And at the livery stable somebody's setting up late and talking.—Yes, it's clearing up. There are the stars—doing their old, old criss-cross journeys in the sky. Scholars haven't settled the matter yet, but they seem to think there are no living beings up there. They're just chalk ... or fire. Only this one is straining away, straining away all the time to make something of itself. The strain's so bad that every sixteen hours everybody lies down and gets a rest.

> *He winds his watch.* *Everybody resting in Grover's Corner*

Hm. ... Eleven o'clock in Grover's Corners.—You get a good rest, too. Good night.

(THE END)

128

GROVER'S CORNERS

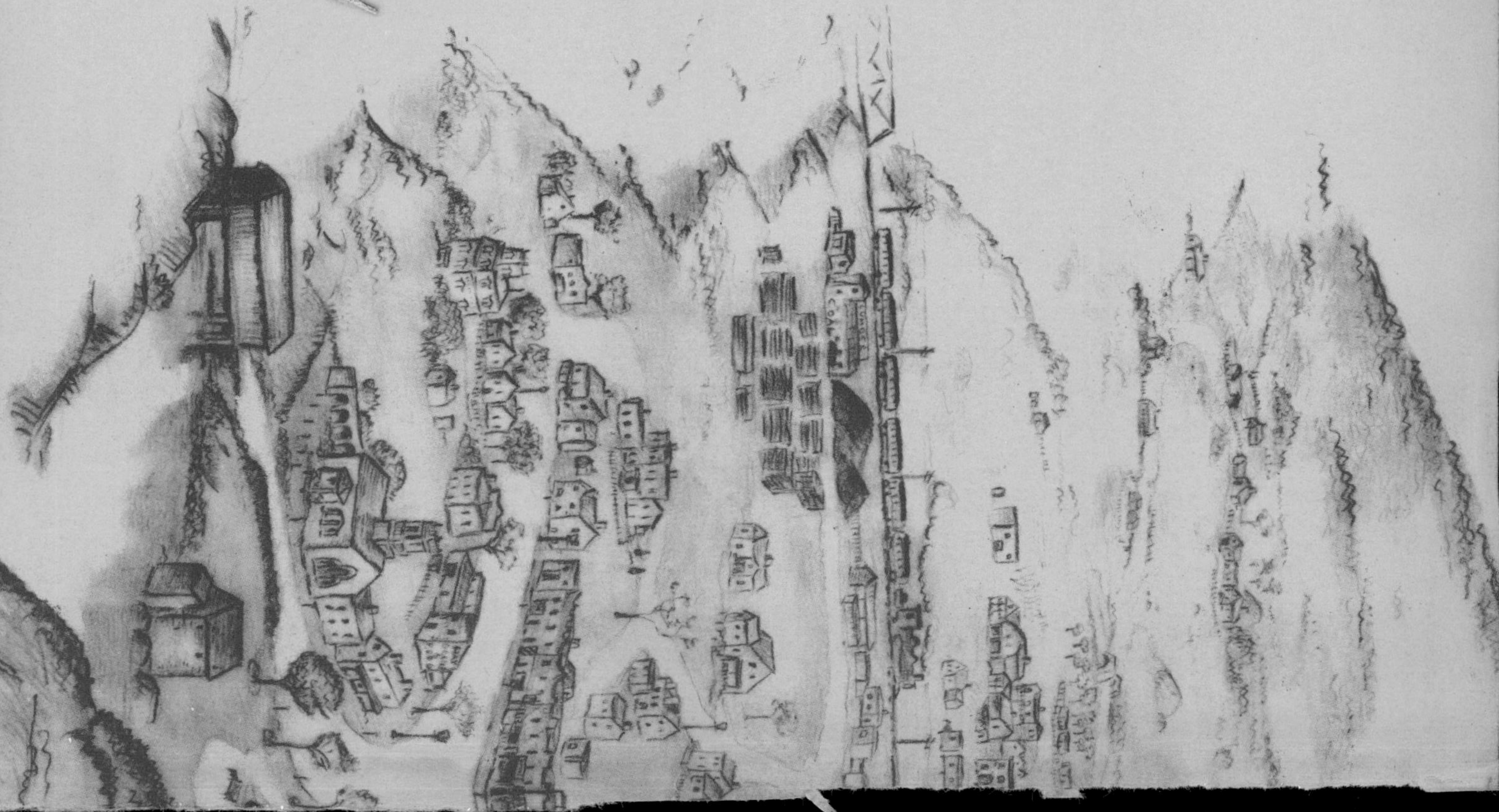